iVAN

A *Screenplay by* SERGEI M. EISENSTEIN

The Terrible

Translated by IVOR MONTAGU *and* HERBERT MARSHALL

Edited by Ivor Montagu, with Appendices and Illustrations

SIMON AND SCHUSTER · NEW YORK · 1962

The co-translators wish to express their thanks and appreciation to Elizabeth Sutherland, whose fertile suggestions, industry and enthusiasm have contributed so much to the qualities of this book.

CONTENTS

INTRODUCTION: EISENSTEIN'S "IVAN"

by
Ivor Montagu

1. THE SCREENPLAY

The screenplay of *Ivan the Terrible* was first published in 1943.* At that time, as is clear from his arrangement of the text, Eisenstein planned to make the film in two parts.

The parts of the film were not made successively. They overlapped in the making, and sequences of both mingled in the floor schedule at Alma-Ata film studios. Part One, however, was finished first, at the end of 1944. It was released at once, and it won applause from the Soviet government and public. The author-director was decorated with the Order of Lenin.

With intensification of actual work the material had developed. At some point, Eisenstein decided to split what had originally been—and is still, of course, in the screenplay printed here—Part Two and to issue nearly the first half of it as a separate section ("Tale Two"—*The Boyars' Plot*), leaving the remainder, the later sequences, to form a third part. This second film, however, ready in 1946, was not well received by the authorities. A scathing comment on it was made in a Party decision published about another film,† and the result was that "Tale Two" did not reach the public until thirteen years later.

Eisenstein was seriously ill in 1947. At the time of his death in 1948 he was working on the completion of the final section. He died of heart failure at the desk of the library in his home in Potilikha, the Moscow film suburb.

---

* *See* Bib. (10).
† *See* Bib. (28).

7

Four reels of the last section are said to have been finished, but they have disappeared.

The screenplay is, therefore, the only form in which it is possible to appreciate the grand design of one of the most remarkable works ever conceived —and so nearly realized—in the cinema.

The *Ivan* screenplay has a double interest. On the one hand it is, in itself, an intensely exciting and vivid dramatic narrative. On the other it provides an opportunity to study an act' of filmic creation; it sheds light not only on its author-director's method of working but on the "cinematic process" in general.

There are no other full Eisenstein scripts accessible to the reader at present. There are fragments, worked out for his classes at the State Institute of Cinematography, Moscow (G.I.K.). There are more elementary sketches, such as those of *Ferghana Canal* (abandoned) and the Mexican film (never finished). The script of *Nevsky* is said to have survived, but the booklet published in the U.S.S.R. as a script of *Potemkin* is nothing of the kind; it is only a transcript made afterward from the finished, edited film. The scenarios written in Hollywood for Paramount by Eisenstein, Grisha Alexandrov, and myself from Blaise Cendrars' *Sutter's Gold* and Theodore Dreiser's *An American Tragedy* could not be published at the time because of copyright obstacles; though they illuminate another aspect of the director's creative work, it should be remembered that they are not original film stories but adaptations from novels. The *Ivan* screenplay stands alone.

Eisenstein taught that a screenplay should be as readable as any other form of literature. He did not work from a scenario bespattered with technical instructions—C.U., pan, location—together with shot numbers. These things would appear finally on some copies, no doubt, but only as a part of the administrative schedule for those whom they directly concerned. He held that a scenario should vividly convey to a reader the feeling, the atmosphere, the emotion of each scene, exactly as these would be perceived and appreciated by the spectator of the finished film. "Literary" scripts without scene numbers are also to be found as a stage in the work of other film directors; indeed, a special term applies to them—the "line-by-line continuity." But in *Ivan* Eisenstein goes much further. Not only does each "scene" (the "scene" sometimes later being a single shot, sometimes an edited group of shots) appear as a separate paragraph, but the paragraphs themselves are scrupulously divided into lines, almost in the manner of free verse, and the order of the words within each line also has a deliberate significance. All this meticulous arrangement was designed to convey not only action and mood but even the future graphic style—to give the reader an inkling of the succession in which the various elements of the described action or scene must be apprehended by the spectator from the future visual composition in order that the dramatic development should fall exactly into place.

The prime object of such a scenario was, of course, to provide a means of complete understanding of the author-director's purpose on the part of his creative colleagues (the actors, cameramen, composer, sound recordist, set and costume designers, makeup men, and assistants in every technical branch). But an incidental by-product, as it were, of the process was that a work became available equally capable of appealing to the dramatic sensibility of the lay reader. This was why Eisenstein was able to publish the script as a piece of literature while shooting was in progress, and why it remains fascinating today.

Eisenstein also held that the director should possess a modicum of drawing ability. The director did not need, he told his pupils, to be a talented graphic artist. But what a director could not visualize sufficiently clearly himself to sketch, or show as a diagram indicating the essential even if only in conventional symbols, he would never be able to describe sufficiently clearly in words for the guidance of his colleagues. His own sketches,* the reader will judge from the examples in this book, went far beyond this minimum. For *Ivan* he produced countless drawings. He himself describes how they arose, not as illustrations for an already thought-out scenario, but as part of the thinking-out, the creative process, itself. They arose before the writing, inspiring parts of it; simultaneously with the writing; and after it, contributing to the intensifying and polishing process. Many are well known. Selections have been published, and collections have been exhibited in Warsaw, Paris, and elsewhere. The interest for us of the samples printed here is to make his method more evident.

More drawings still, and innumerable jotted notes, appear on the reverse blank pages and in the margins of his own personal copy of the script. Their study brightly illumines the continuous process of perfecting with which Eisenstein, to the last moment and beyond, incessantly deepened the content of his treatment, loaded it with more and more significant detail, gilded refined gold. Once, when I was young and naïve, I put to Sergei Mikhailovich this question: Should a director complete his script precisely and then shoot exactly what is written, or should he write it approximately and then modify it on the floor? I say "naïve" because the answer I received now seems to me obvious: at every stage of his realization of the film he should be ready to make use of everything, even the unexpected, consistent with its idea. Nikolskaya, in her absorbing article,† finds places where the many-times-corrected script was realized exactly, places where it was changed still more upon the floor. That Eisenstein's creative demon never froze in preconceived positions but was ever alert to seize each happy "happenstance" is sufficiently attested by his felicitous decision in *Potemkin* to locate its massacre scene on the Odessa steps (where none of the massacres of those days actually happened, although he created it so vividly that it has now entered illegitimately into history) and by the wonderful use made by him, Grisha Alexandrov and Eduard Tisse, of the mist in Odessa roadstead in the same film.

* "My Drawings," p. 301.
† *See* Bib. (32).

9

Consistent with its idea—those are the crucial and difficult watchwords. To admit an improvisation, to improve safely by however painstaking an accretion and refinement of detail—these need the rigid will and unwavering power of visualization of a chess grand master. Where Eisenstein transgressed, with this very film, in respect to its general idea, we shall see below. To his visualizing power, nevertheless, this script and the two completed films bear conclusive witness. In sequence after sequence, scene after scene, the words of the scenario bring before our eyes exactly the drama and emotion we derive from sight of what is on the screen. For each of Dombrovsky's stills reproduced in this book, there is an appropriate script phrase that determined its "feeling" as faithfully as a gene prefigures a character.

2. THE STYLE

But if Eisenstein bade the director be ever-ready, like a captain on the battlefield, to suit his dispositions to the lie of the terrain and the sway of combat, like a good captain he was determined to leave the minimum to chance. Scientist no less than artist—or, rather, scientist in art, capable of extraordinary intuitions and sensitivities to form, he was nonetheless perpetually seeking, on his own behalf and that of his pupils, the means of increasing the *conscious* element, the deliberate, in artistic creation. Control must attain the maximum. No hair must lie out of place, unless foreseen and to order.

Unless this is understood, there is risk of missing the whole point of his lifework. Planning a tragedy on the grand scale, Eisenstein chose a form to suit it and plumbed the recesses of the form. When the reels of *Ivan*, Part One, were first screened, not a few admirers were astonished to see in this, the latest work of its director, a period piece, heavily stylized. Was this the master they worshiped, the great innovator who first used nature as the stuff of drama? The inspirer, through *Potemkin*, via Grierson and *Drifters*, of whole schools of "documentary"? The youthful realist who, impatient of theatrical bonds of bricks and mortar, burst out to stage a play of working-class struggle in a real factory and then to do the same on film? The conjuror who pinned and captured first the Russian, then the Mexican, landscape as his back cloth?

Especially, were these actor-puppets with their rolling eyes directed by the great exponent of "typage," the use of non-actors to seek greater realism?

Even to ask these questions is to go astray. The consistency in Eisenstein is the perpetual search to increase the range of elements subject to artistic mastery and to discover the means by which these elements may be made to serve. Perhaps the clue that was forgotten is that the theater the young master and his companions sprang from was really a circus, with clowns' grins and acrobats, a circus of satire. When Eisenstein broke into cinema it was not to retreat into naturalism that he tried the factory setting but in an experiment to recruit the factory among the tractable materials capable of being included within the artist's repertoire. His realism was comprised of symbols whose impact was the greater because they were themselves real.

Eisenstein's recourse to natural settings and types was really antinatural, at the opposite pole from the contemporary (and therefore sometimes confused with his method) Dziga-Vertov theory of the Kino-Eye. Dziga-Vertov's idea was that the artist should interfere as little as possible with natural processes and use the camera only to observe. This is a principle as impossible in art as it is in science. Just as the scientist's observation inevitably interferes, if only by a beam of electrons or a stream of light, and therefore must be allowed for in seeking the truth of the processes he is trying to observe, so the artist, in reproducing nature, however abstemiously intended his interference, is inevitably creating and arbitrating by the act of selection. The Kino-Eye theory—which is but "documentary" taken to its logical limit—is a blind alley, negated by every attempt to explore it. Eisenstein, on the contrary, basing himself on the Engels dictum that freedom is the awareness of necessity, sought the power to re-create a vivid reality by knowledge of the laws and processes of effect within his chosen art. He chose that art precisely because, of all the arts, it gives the possibility of the widest range of subjugable means—graphic composition not only spatially but in time, light, shade, color (in three reels of *Ivan*), music, sound, living beings (actors)—and of subjugating them most plastically—by preplanning and, afterward, by editorial scissors. When Eisenstein dealt with nature, it was not as worshiper but as some magician of old, triumphing over the forces of nature to weave his spells.

To Eisenstein the non-actor was a graphic image of infinite adaptability, with appearance more convincing than the makeup of a professional; editing was the means to use him without having to encounter the stubborn habits instilled by the professional's training. There was no principle about it, only practical advantage, and when he set himself the task of portraying the majesty and tragedy of power, he naturally turned to classicism and, as Bachelis acutely saw,* "the resurrection of the Russian classical style of acting as practiced at the beginning of the 19th century, with its deliberate coldness and its contempt for internal fullness of emotion." It was a reaction against the naturalism—totally unsuited to this theme—of the Moscow Art Theater and a resurrection of that which the Moscow Art Theater had initially been a reaction against. To quote Bachelis again, "The magnificent Byzantine ceremonies portrayed are not merely the decorative luxury of an operatic-historical production; solemnity, pomp, majesty and picturesque wealth are the necessary concomitants of the very idea of the film."

3. THE THEME

"The very idea of the film . . ." This, chosen by Eisenstein, was no less than the birth of the Russian state, the attempt by a renaissance monarch to

* *See* Bib. (24).

construct a unitary power for the nation, above and replacing the rulers of petty feudal princedoms—the boyars—among whom the Grand Duke had been hitherto but primus inter pares. Such a task required review of the traditional literary image of Ivan.

This is how Eisenstein himself wrote about Ivan:*

> Making this film was an extremely complicated matter. The personality of Ivan the Terrible and his historic role had to be thoroughly reconsidered. Ivan the IV's principal aim was to create a strong centralized sovereign State in place of the scattered, mutually hostile feudal principalities of old Russia. He laid the foundations of a vast and mighty power. . . . The heirs to the feudal lords crushed by Ivan refused to accept the idea of a unified power and did not scruple to resort to treachery and conspiracy. They secretly prepared the ground for an invasion of Russia by her western neighbors and it was they who cried to heaven about the cruelty and bloodthirstiness of the Moscow Tsar. They painted Ivan's harsh measures and relentless firmness in protecting the interests of the State against the self-interest and arbitrary power of the boyars as irrational malice and insane thirst for blood. . . . Their writings determined the past historical and artistic interpretation of the role and character of Ivan but they were far from being unbiased pictures of "things gone by." They were deliberate propaganda designed to incite hatred against the Moscow State and to discredit it among Western nations.

Is this idea of Ivan historical? Yes, certainly. No one, seeing the film, could conceive of it as a whitewashing operation. But Eisenstein's Ivan is no monster, no special "Thing from the Slav Renaissance." Just as at Paramount in Hollywood Eisenstein had accepted to be interested in the one modern American murder story—Dreiser's—that links the crime-committer through his growth, makeup and background to the social influences around him, so here he—in Grisha's words—"shows how Ivan's character was made 'terrible' by his environment," i.e., his role and situation.† It is not only a Marxist interpretation but also nowadays a commonplace of academic historians that the unification of the State by monarchy was everywhere a progressive stage in national development. This story was always bloody. Bachelis‡ does well to remind us that in Western Europe the classic authority for the prince's duty during this process was Machiavelli, and Eisenstein at the very outset of his script (page 24) challengingly recalls the persons and events contemporary with the "Terrible" in other lands. It is known that Ivan was a milder man before he lost Anastasia. (Thereafter, his matrimonial adventures, spared to us in this film study, matched those of Henry VIII.) It is true also that the principal sources for the traditional image that has come down of Ivan are

---

* See Bib. (11). Ivan the Terrible (1530-1584) was Ivan the IV of Muscovy.
† See Bib. (23).
‡ See Bib. (24).

his lengthy correspondence with Kurbsky, the latter ever seeking to justify his betrayal; Staden, who spied on him for his enemies; and the scribes of those boyars who, on his death, returned to Moscow as puppets with the armies of the Polish King.* Expect as well to find a balanced picture of Richard Crookshank in Shakespeare's "historie" written to do pleasure to a Tudor Queen, or, for that matter, of Henry VIII in a chronicle written by a dispossessed monk.

Shaw in *Saint Joan* depicts, intellectually, the birth among the masses of the national idea and embodies it in the argy-bargy of contrasting characters. Eisenstein in *Ivan* depicts the institutional conflicts attending national birth and embodies them in a graphic study of the torment within the monarch, a child of his times, his vision of duty warring with his ties of loyalty to kin and church. He personalizes this conflict in subtle, ingeniously interwoven relationships and seemingly fated developments, sometimes bloodcurdling, always grandiose.

Here is how the director explains the relation of theme and form: †

> The grandeur of our subject called for monumental means of presentation. Details were pushed into the background and everything was subordinated to the principal idea of the might of Russia and the struggle to make it a great power. The principal conflicts in the general struggle, in which Ivan lost those who were nearest and dearest to him—some because, failing to understand his aims, they turned away from him, some because the mercenary nature of their own aims caused them to oppose him, and some because they perished at his side in the course of the struggle—called for the use of the forms of tragedy.
>
> This was how the style of the film was determined, a style that runs counter to many of the traditional methods to which we have grown accustomed on the screen both here and abroad. The general custom is to try to make the historical personage, the historical hero, "accessible," to portray him as an ordinary person showing the ordinary, human traits of other people, to show him, as it is said, "in dressing-gown and slippers."
>
> But with Ivan we wanted a different tone. In him we wished chiefly to convey a sense of majesty, and this led us to adopt majestic forms. Frequently the dialogue is accompanied by music, and choral singing intermingles with it. The principal idea—the formation of a strong State—governs the Tsar's whole conduct.
>
> Irrelevant details in the characters of the other personages are ignored, while their principal features—chiefly their hostility or loyalty to Ivan's cause—are drawn in bold relief. Because of this, when taken individually some of the characters may perhaps seem somewhat one-sided. But the point is that they must be taken together

* At the close of the opera *Boris Godunov.*
† *See* Bib. (11).

as a whole, in their general relationship to the cause for which Ivan stands. They cannot be taken separately, just as the part of one instrument cannot be singled out in judging a whole complex orchestrated score, for the meaning of their individual actions is disclosed only in their general interaction. Neither can they be considered outside the plastic setting and musical whole in which they are immersed.

The threads of the interrelationships of which Eisenstein speaks together form a dynamically developing dramatic tapestry. Details, at the time appearing insignificant or else justified merely by service as color to an early scene, emerge later as in fact seeds of growth that powerfully determine the subsequent action. In the script, the theme is fully triumphant, Eisenstein's objective is attained.

Where the whole thing came a cropper in practice was through the circumstance of its conception as two films and, yet further, its development as three. Stubborn problems arise from the very nature of sequel presentation in the cinema. The audience cannot turn back a page, from Part Two to Part One, as a reader of the scenario can while it is printed as a book. Feature sequels in film viewing are known, if rarely, both in the U.S.S.R. and elsewhere, but the greatest success in this kind is with such as *Pather Panchali* and its successors and the Gorki or *Maxim* trilogies—or, for that matter, the adventures of Tarzan or the various offspring of *Dracula*—where each subject is independent in itself and the unifying factor is simply a character or characters, each time hopping onward into a quite separate locality or period. A continuous plot is just not possible.

When the sum of the projected series is a unity, the development and balance of the whole so carefully studied, as in *Ivan*, then obstacles of Himalayan magnitude immediately obstruct the separations. Examine here our screenplay. Has there ever been a more preposterous remark than that on page 268 introducing the Vogt of Weissenstein? "Sometime—long ago—he came with an embassy to the young Ivan, and spectators will remember him from the prologue of the film." Will they, indeed? Perhaps on rare occasions all three parts of the triple film might have been revived together for galas and festivals, so that hardy spectators with powerful *Sitzfleisch* might see the thing through as long as they could put up with it, like the Wagnerian "Ring," but 99 and a large decimal point of spectators would have been seeing in the Vogt a figure that last appeared to them (if ever) not merely 200 odd pages but two or three years before.

A similar lost echo would have been the reappearance of Foma and Yeroma, grown "handsome, bearded," toward the end of Part Three.

The script envisages one dramatic curtain at the end of Part One, and the obvious choice for an eventual second break was where Eisenstein finally put it, after the defeat of the Staritskys. Yet even this involved him in serious dramatic difficulties. To omit the Prologue from the beginning of Part One weakened our understanding there of Ivan's conduct; we had advance knowledge only by hearsay of the bitterness of the boyar struggle that conditioned its harshness; we did not see its origin with our own eyes, a proof so much stronger. Yet it had to be transferred to Part Two, where the separation of the family intrigue part of the story made it still more necessary and appropriate. The awful oprichnik oath at the end of Part One (in the script) is a perfect introduction to the Tsar's return at the start of Part Two, where he is embittered by betrayal and the loss of his loved one. But when the oath is removed as an excrescence to the film of Part One considered on its own, the opening venom of "Tale Two," now separated from its cause, comes as a shock to the spectator, who left Ivan noble and suffering and sees him suddenly return transformed and violent. Further, with the second curtain placed, as it was, after the defeat of the Staritskys, how could Eisenstein, having omitted from "Tale Two" the there irrelevant beginning of the Eustace story, have built it up later so as to retain its climax in the Confession Sequence? Such questions can now never be answered; but is it not here, in the asperities consequent on the breaking of the whole into parts, in the consequent changes of proportion and balance, that we find the rock on which the project foundered?

Hindsight often gives the explanation nowadays that "Tale Two" contained topical allusions about ruthlessness that the authorities found too near the mark. But this leaves everything unexplained. Why swallow the script and not its embodiment? It is quite clear that a crude analogy may be drawn between Russia's problems in Ivan's day and Eisenstein's. The struggle to build a strong state, the pressure of external foes seeking to foment treasonous partnerships within and the consequent suspicions—these parallels were inherent in the subject. We know from Eisenstein's preliminary studies, and from the internal structure of the film itself, how scrupulously the author-director sought the essence of the *period* factors. Naturally, a creative artist interpreting the past to his contemporaries reflects, in proportion to his integrity, his own experience of the world and man. But that the task Eisenstein consciously set himself was in no sense a veiled (as Lenin called it, "Ethiopian") criticism but something quite different is attested by the dates. The film was made from 1943 to 1945, at the height of the war. It will forever be a wonder, a tribute to the tenacity and firmness of vision of the author-director on the one hand and the liberality of the authorities and administrators toward a never complaisant artist on the other, that, with the Nazis at the gates of Stalingrad, with the entire country mobilized to resist the frightful wounds inflicted upon it, facilities could be afforded for a lavish reconstruction of renaissance Moscow in the heart of Central Asia. *But this is because the film was a grand patriotic demonstration for the Great Patriotic War*—a film about "an heroic builder of our State," to use Eisenstein's own words.* That Eisenstein so saw it, we know from his whole approach to the film and everything he wrote about it. The preparatory work was begun around 1940, all undoubtedly a part of that preparation of the Soviet people for the ordeal gathering

* *See* Bib. (11).

against them in the west, of which *Nevsky* was likewise a part and in which many other talented film makers participated. Such modern parallels as may be detected between the strains and stresses of the times and those of Ivan's day were no bootleg introductions but always implicit in the parallels of the situation, explicit in the script—approved by the authorities and widely published beforehand. "Tale Two" is exactly as its author-director left it; that nothing was smuggled in can be confirmed at once by comparison of published text and finished film. The only fresh topical allusions are still further patriotic ones, e.g., the new opening title to Part One,* the enlarged speech by King Sigismund of Poland to his court,† and the new terminal color sequence to "Tale Two."‡

But if there were no new introductions to provoke objection, what then led to the fiasco?

H. G. Wells left us a brilliant short story about a rajah and a ranee, who loved each other with a love sung by poets, a perfect love. In the flower of their youth together, the princess was bitten in the foot by a serpent and she died. The rajah resolved to raise above her tomb a marble palace so majestic and so beautiful that it should outshine the Taj (unless, perchance, it was itself the Taj) and make his love for her immortal. For years and years he labored, with a regiment of architects and an army of artificers. At last the shrine was complete. Yet something was wrong; something—he could not tell what—marred the perfection of its symmetry. At last, head on one side, he decided. The culprit was an object in the corner. Pointing to the tomb, he cried: "Take that damn thing away!" This sad parable is an epitome of formalism.

Something like this happened with Eisenstein and *Ivan*. His critics—and this does not diminish him; it only defines him—have sometimes called him "the master of the episode." Meaning that he was apt to deepen and to polish the episode so thoroughly that, while in itself it became a thing of brilliance, it was apt to become hypertrophied in its relationship with the whole. It is noteworthy that the two most perfectly balanced unities among Eisenstein films—*Potemkin* and "Tale Two"—are both polished and inflated episodes, originally conceived as parts of greater wholes.§ The Party decision on *The Great Life*, with the backhanded swipe at Eisenstein, which so long delayed the release of "Tale Two," complained—among other things—that therein the director had shown the oprichniks as a band of degenerates similar to the Ku Klux Klan and Ivan as a waverer "something like Hamlet." Can anyone deny this? Ivan of the grand design, taken from start to finish of the original script, is a man of inflexible purpose, of iron will. The oprichniks are clearly the men of the people, rough and liable to corruption maybe, but

* P. 288.
† P. 296.
‡ P. 300.
§ *Potemkin* was originally to have been only a sequence in a big film, *1905*, the rest of which was never made.

plainly gathered by the Tsar to serve as his ring against feudal kin and external foe. But boiled down into "Tale Two"? Had the author not become so devoted to the polishing of his chip of diamond—till it shines as a deeply felt personal horror story of brilliance unparalleled—that he had compromised its functional role? He himself so described the trouble. He wrote (using a different simile): "Like a bad foundryman, we light-mindedly allowed the precious stream of creation to be poured out over sand and become disposed in private unessential sidelines." * Even the title chosen—no longer *Ivan, Part II*, but a tale in itself, *The Boyars' Plot*—showed how much the master plan had narrowed.

The answer to a question that has puzzled many devotees of Eisenstein throws light on the way even graphic qualities enhanced this contraction. Why did Eisenstein modify his lifelong exclusive partnership with Tisse? Yurenyev† tells us that he chose to use *two* cameramen, Eduard Tisse for exteriors only and Moskvin for interiors, precisely because he wished the plastic contrast of two visions, two entirely different seeing and composing eyes, to emphasize (unconsciously, graphically) the duality in Ivan's mind and conscience—the clear exteriors where the future dominated, his progressive role as the creator of the nation-state, reliant on the people for victory in the conflict; and the oppressive, cruel interiors, where the barbarism of the feudal past woke echoes in his own nature, kin of kin to the boyars. This duality is apparent in Part One, but all the scenes that were to have been Tisse's share in Part Two are in the latter half, or among the sections pared from *The Boyars' Plot*; with them even the visual associations displaying the social meaning of the conflict vanish and only the horrors of the internecine feud remain.

Why did he let this happen? Eisenstein was no fool, he was one of the most acute minds of his day. He must have foreseen the obstacles. But he was a man of boundless integrity, invincible courage, implacable stubbornness, wherever his passion for perfect presentation of what he saw as truth might lead.

So "Tale Two," no longer a cutting tool within the grand design but a dark jewel on its own, became his final masterpiece as *Potemkin* was his first. Timeous but untimely, for the times were out of joint. A legacy that lay hidden for thirteen years.

However, the grandeur of the original conception is still here, in the screenplay.

* *See* Bib. (19).
† *See* Bib. (36).

The Screenplay

List of Principal Characters*

OF THE PROLOGUE:

IVAN IV, *Grand Prince of Muscovy*

HELENA GLINSKY, *his mother*

PRINCE TELEPNEV-OBOLENSKY

BOYAR SHUISKY

BOYAR BYELSKY

KASPAR VON OLDENBOCK, *the Ambassador of the Livonian Order*

HIS SECRETARY

THE AMBASSADOR OF THE HANSEATIC LEAGUE

IVAN'S NURSE

* The actors playing these roles, together with all other credits, are listed in the back of this book under "Notes on the Film Transcripts."

OF THE STORY:

IVAN IV, *Tsar of Muscovy*

ANASTASIA ROMANOVNA (ZAKHARIN), *his wife*

MALYUTA SKURATOV-BYELSKY (GREGORY)

ALEXEY BASMANOV

FYODOR BASMANOV (FEDKA), *his son*

FOMA *and* YEROMA CHOKHOV, *plebeians*

OSIP NEPEYA, *the Tsar's Ambassador to the English Court*

PRINCE ANDREW KURBSKY

AMBROGIO, *his secretary*

BOYAR KOLYCHEV, *afterwards* PHILIP, *Metropolitan of Moscow*

EUSTACE, *his acolyte*

PIMEN, *at first Metropolitan of Moscow, later Archbishop of*
Novgorod

PETER VOLYNETS, *his acolyte*

EUPHROSYNE STARITSKY, *Ivan's aunt*

VLADIMIR STARITSKY, *her son*

PENINSKY, *an old boyar, of the Staritsky faction*

DEMYAN TESHATA, *a Staritsky bondsman*

NIKOLA, *a beggar simpleton*

ENGINEER RASMUSSEN

HENRYK STADEN, *a German mercenary*

QUEEN ELIZABETH I OF ENGLAND

KING SIGISMUND OF POLAND

THE JESTER OF KING SIGISMUND, *German agent at his court*

KASPAR VON OLDENBOCK, *the Ambassador of the Livonian Order,*
now Vogt of Weissenstein Castle

IVAN THE TERRIBLE

PART ONE

pROLOGUE

THE APPROACHING STORM

Clouds surge across the screen.

Voices chant:
> *Black clouds*
> *Are gathering,*
> *Crimson blood*
> *Bathes the dawn.*

Lightning flashes.
Thunder roars.

Voices chant:
> *Cunning treason—*
> *From the boyars—*
> *To royal power*
> *Offers battle.*

Summoned by the lightning, the title of the film appears:

IVAN THE TERRIBLE.

23

The clouds billow.
Against the background of the clouds, the credits pass slowly across the
screen.
Voices chant:
> *Now comes the time*
> *Of dire conflict,*
> *Guard and save*
> *The soil of Rus*—*
> *A prize attracting*
> *Fierce plunderers—*
> *Spare neither sire nor mother*
> *For the sake of the great Russian realm.*

The titles pass.

Voices chant:
> *A cloud is risen*
> *Dread and black.*
> *Now the time is at hand*
> *To swear to Rus*
> *A weighty oath,*
> *A fearful oath.*

Through pealing thunder the voices chant:
> *Preserve the realm,*
> *Stand for Moscow,*
> *Guard the city.*
> *On the bones of its foes*
> *From the four corners of the earth*
> *The Russian realm shall rise.*

An introductory title rises into view—
As it passes, there swells beneath it
Tsar Ivan's musical theme,
"The Approaching Storm"—

IN THAT SAME CENTURY THAT SAW IN EUROPE
CHARLES V AND PHILIP II,
CATHERINE DE' MEDICI AND THE DUKE OF ALBA,
HENRY VIII AND BLOODY MARY,
THE FIRES OF THE INQUISITION AND THE NIGHT OF ST. BARTHOLOMEW,

---

* The name, in Ivan's time, for the Russian dominion. Among the petty Grand Duke-
doms that composed it then, that of Muscovy gradually achieved ascendancy and became known as Moscow Rus, later as only Rus, and eventually as Russia.

To the Throne of the Grand Princes of Muscovy
Came he who first became
Tsar and Autocrat of All Rus
Tsar
Ivan the Terrible.

The theme of Ivan reaches its climax
Black clouds envelope the screen . . .
Through the darkness surge the voices:

> *Black clouds are spreading,*
> *Crimson blood bathes the dawn.*
> *On the bones of its foes,*
> *In the hot ash of fires,*
> *Rus, one and united,*
> *Is welded together.*

A sudden clap of thunder.
The music ceases abruptly.

QUICK FADE-IN

THE HALL OF DARKNESS

In the gloom a bright spot of light picks out
an eight-year-old boy, crouching fearfully in a corner.

The camera approaches him swiftly.
C l o s e - u p—the frightened face of the boy.
O f f s c r e e n—the anguished scream of a woman.
The boy creeps out of view.

The boy crouched on the floor.
Over the boy pass the shadows of people,
Walking by with tapers.

A low door opens suddenly.
A sharp ray of light cuts into the hall.
In the light comes running, then drops beside the boy,
a woman in the garb of a princess.

The Princess is beside the boy. She speaks in feverish haste:

I am dying . . . they've poisoned me . . . Beware poison! . . .
Beware the boyars! . . .

Girls rush in, seize hold of the Princess.
They take her back into her chamber. The door slams to.

It is dark once more. The terrified boy.
A harsh voice in the darkness:
The Grand Princess Helena Glinsky is no more.
A hubbub of women's voices.

At the top of the staircase. A voice shouts in the darkness.
Seize Telepnev-Obolensky!
Feet running in the darkness.
Down the staircase is dragged handsome Telepnev-Obolensky.
Two or three men holding aloft tapers.

At the bottom of the stairs Telepnev-Obolensky wrenches himself free.
He rushes toward the door leading to the Princess' chamber.

Emerging bent, through the door, appears and then towers like a rock in
                                      his path
a boyar of gigantic stature (Andrew Shuisky).
Telepnev leaps aside, away from the boyar.

The voice out of the darkness:
Strangle the Princess' lover!
Telepnev flings himself to one side.
He sees the boy.
He throws himself down at the feet of the boy:
Save me, Grand Prince of Moscow!

Telepnev is seized and dragged away from the feet of Ivan.
Telepnev desperately clutching at the thin small legs
of the Grand Prince.

From above, the harsh voice—Andrew Shuisky's.
TAKE HIM AWAY!

Telepnev is dragged to a flight of stairs leading downward.
He is beaten and kicked.
His silk shirt is torn open.

Torches moving downward.
Telepnev being dragged to the dungeons.

The tapers disappear upstairs.
The torches downstairs . . .

The boy Ivan trembling alone in the darkness.

FADE OUT

FADE IN

THE HALL OF AUDIENCE

Many people. An atmosphere of solemn expectancy. Boyars.

Above the throne—a fresco:
the Angel of Wrath—from the Apocalypse—
trampling the universe underfoot.

The throne of the Grand Prince
as yet empty.

The boyars sitting in groups on low forms.
They are talking among themselves.
Explanations to the uninitiated:
The Grand Prince in person will receive the Ambassadors.
We shall hear which Moscow has decided to pay.
Hansa, or Livonia.

They glance sideways at the ambassadors.
They point them out to one another.

Apart, in two groups, stand the foreign embassies.
The representative of the Livonian Order—Kaspar von Oldenbock,
a knight in a white mantle that reaches to the floor.
Beside him his secretary, a Humanist,
looking like Erasmus of Rotterdam,
with an astute and cunning face.

Heading the other group—a red-bearded merchant,
looking like a sea robber,
the representative of the Hanseatic League
of German Merchant Cities.

Von Oldenbock and the red-bearded merchant
looking each other up and down with hostile glances.

The Humanist smiles to himself a thin-lipped smile.

The Hall of Audience is packed with people.
A general movement.
The embassies draw themselves up.

The door opens.
High-ranking boyars enter. Bodyguards.
Palace Guards.
P A N: from the door, through the hall,
toward the throne of the Grand Prince
in the midst of his suite comes the thin boy Ivan,
clad in full Grand Prince's robes.
He is thirteen years old.
His skinny neck protrudes from a massive gold collar.
His eyes are wide open. Fear lurks in them.
He walks timidly between the ranks of the boyars.
As he passes, all drop to their knees.

One on either side of the throne,
Andrew Shuisky and Byelsky,
make deep obeisance to him.

Ivan hesitatingly approaches the throne.
He is guided toward it.
He is seated on it.

At a sign the ambassadors approach.
Each bends the knee.

Everyone is kneeling before Ivan.

In fear and confusion the tiny Ivan gazes
at the assembled boyars prostrate at his feet.
At the ambassadors each with bended knee.

And, in mortal terror, he carefully and distinctly pronounces
—at a sign from Shuisky—the words of the ceremonial proclamation:
We, by the Grace of God, Ioannis Basildis,
Magnus Moscovitae Rerum Dux,
Voluntatem Nostrum Proclamemus . . .

As one, the boyars rise to their feet.
Their tall caps increase their stature.
The ambassadors stand up, bowing respectfully.

Ivan on the throne.
His skinny neck projects like a blade of grass through the heavy gold
collar.
His child's eyes are opened wide.

But all the pomp is beginning to affect him:
gradually his timidity is leaving him.
The boy settles more firmly on the throne.

Byelsky solemnly announces:
Ivan son of Vasily, Grand Prince of Moscow . . .
All bow.
. . . deems it well to enter into a trading agreement with,
and to make payment for the right of passage of wares through the Baltic
to,
the Hanseatic League of German Merchant Cities.

At a sign from Byelsky,
to the red-bearded Hansa merchant
there approaches a scribe
bearing a scroll and seal.

The Hansa merchant stretches out his hand for the scroll.
The movement is arrested by the rap of Andrew Shuisky's iron staff.

Shuisky announces loudly:
Ivan son of Vasily, Grand Prince of Moscow, has reconsidered:
the trading agreement will be entered into with the Livonian Order of
Sword Bearers.

And at a sign from Shuisky there appears a second scribe,
with an identical scroll and seal,
who hastily goes over with it to Kaspar von Oldenbock.

The old Humanist beside him quickly takes the scroll
and hides it
in the folds of his black gown.

General astonishment.

Byelsky shouts excitedly at Shuisky:
Hansa! The German Hansa!
The Privy Council decided definitely on Hansa!

Shuisky:
The will of the Grand Prince can alter even the decisions of the Privy
Council!

Byelsky:
But the Sovereign's word was actually given . . .

Shuisky:
The Grand Prince is sole master of his word.
At his will it is given, at his will it is altered.
The Grand Prince's will is law!

Byelsky is furious.
Tears of rage stand in his eyes.
But the will of the Grand Prince gave the decision to the German Hansa!

The boy Ivan fidgets on his throne.
He evidently does not like others to speak in his name.
It is obvious that on this particular subject
he has an opinion of his own.

In the frightened boy the eaglet awakens.
He wishes to speak.

But Shuisky does not let him.
Again he speaks on the boy's behalf.
The will of the Grand Prince extends license to the Livonian Order.

From amongst the boyars a loud voice exclaims in envy:
Shuisky has been paid a high price! . . .

A cunning smile appears on the face of the secretary to the Livonian
Ambassador.
A furious glare appears on the face of the Hansa merchant.

Byelsky splutters, choking with wrath.
Shrilly he tries to shout something.

Ivan wants to speak.

But Andrew Shuisky raps fiercely with his iron staff.
He solemnly declares:
Ivan son of Vasily, Grand Prince of Moscow,
is wearied by the affairs of embassy.
He therefore deems this audience at an end.

Byelsky attempts to protest.
But . . .
Shuisky outshouts him:
The Grand Prince's will is law!

Once more he raps with his iron staff.
And once more all prostrate themselves before Ivan.
All make humble obeisance to Ivan.

The legs of Ivan dangle helplessly from the throne.
They swing about:
they cannot reach the floor. . . .

They cannot reach until beneath the feet of the Grand Prince of Moscow
is placed the desired footstool.

And above the Prince of Moscow
the Angel of Wrath—
from the Apocalypse—
tramples the universe underfoot.

FADE OUT

FADE IN

IVAN'S APARTMENTS

Sing about the ocean! The ocean!—
cries Ivan merrily, running around in his bedchamber.

Lifting high the skirts of his Grand-Prince's robe,
he hops about on one leg.
He is all haste to divest himself of his robes, taking them off as he moves.

His old nurse and two nursemaids-of-the-bedchamber
help Ivan to disrobe.
The boy is impatient to get out of his gold collar.
In a cracked voice the old nurse sings:
> *Ocean-sea,*
> *Azure sea,*
> *Azure sea,*
> *Glorious sea . . .*

Ivan takes off his Grand-Prince's cap:
> *Thy waters reach to the very Heavens,*
> *Thy waves roll up to the sun on high . . .*
Ivan throws off the heavy collar of beaten gold.
He is listening.
And thinking.
> *. . . the rivers of Rus*
> *they flow to thee.*
> *By thy shores*
> *stand mighty cities . . .*
Thinking hard, Ivan stares in front of him.
He ceases disrobing.
The song has gripped him.
> *The cities that stand there*
> *were ours of old.*
> *By black foes*
> *they're now enthralled . . .*
A number of boyars enter noisily.
Fierce argument is in progress.

Byelsky leaps around Shuisky, snapping and snarling:
We must make a pact with the Hanseatic League!
Shuisky replies menacingly:
We shall make a pact with the Livonians!

The old woman continues disrobing Ivan.
Her song is barely audible:

> *. . . Ocean-sea,*
> *Azure sea,*
> *Azure sea,*
> *Russian sea . . .*

Shuisky roughly interrupts the song:
How dare you disturb the boy with that rubbish?
Get out!

The old woman hastily makes her exit through the private chapel.
Ivan gazes longingly after her.
He looks up frowningly at Shuisky.
Byelsky keeps pressing his point:
It would be better to pay the Hansa merchants!
Shuisky sticks to his:
We're going to pay the Livonians!

Ivan's disrobing is almost complete.
The nursemaids remove the last of his ceremonial attire.
Underneath—Ivan has on a simple shirt.
Almost poor.
But in the eyes of the listening Ivan
there lurks something
of that look that came to him upon the throne.

Shuisky and Byelsky never pause:
A deal with Hansa would be better for the State!
Better, not for the State—but for you!
And you've been bought by the Livonians!

Byelsky screams shrilly:
We must pay Hansa!

We shall pay the Livonians,—
answers Shuisky.

Amidst the richly-clad boyars
Ivan looks almost poverty-stricken.
But his voice rings out pridefully:
It's no obligation of ours to pay tribute to anyone!
Our grandsires built those cities on the coast.
That soil is properly part of our heritage—
they must belong to Moscow.

Shuisky says sneeringly:
Nobody's going to be stupid enough to give back those cities!
Possession is nine points of the law,—
Byelsky in servile fashion rallies to his opponent.

Says Ivan:
If they do not yield them willingly—we'll take them by force!

Everyone laughs.

SHUISKY:
By force?
BYELSKY:
Where's your force coming from?

The might of Rus, that you have squandered!
That has trickled away into boyar pockets!—
shouts Ivan.

All roar with laughter.

Shuisky, overcome with laughing,
drops into a low armchair:
I shall die! . . . *God Almighty!*
He flings his feet onto the bed.

Ivan jumps forward.
Panting with anger,
he shouts:
Take your feet off that bed!
Take them off, I say!
Take your feet off my mother's bed!

Between his teeth he adds:
. . . my mother, whom you curs worried to death!

I'm a cur, eh?—
Shuisky roars, rising from his chair like a wild beast:
She was a bitch herself!
That He-dog Telepnev and she were thick together;
no one knows who sired you!

The gigantic figure of Shuisky towers over Ivan,
brandishing his iron staff:
Son of a bitch!

Ivan covers his head with his arms to ward off the blow,
then suddenly,
unexpectedly even to himself,
he screams out hysterically:
ARREST HIM!

All,
and Ivan among them,
are staggered with surprise.
The other boyars shrink towards the door.
Shuisky stands as though petrified.

Ivan searches with his eyes.
At the entrance to his private chapel he notices his kennelmen.
They too are standing motionless.

And now with a voice of decision, Ivan commands:
Take him away!

And . . . the kennelmen take hold of the chief lord of the realm—
                                        Andrew Shuisky.
They hustle him from the apartment.

The rest of the boyars make themselves scarce, muttering fearfully:
The Elder Boyar given over to the kennel lackeys!
Ivan remains alone.

39

He is frightened by his own determination
and by the unexpectedness of everything that has happened.

His strength leaves him.
He is once more a weak, helpless little boy.

He presses his face against the covers on his mother's bed
and sobs as though his head lay on her breast.
His skinny shoulders shake.

Hurried footsteps are heard in the corridor.
The door creaks.

Ivan cowers, afraid to turn around.

Through the door, fearfully comes one of the kennelmen.
Cautiously he touches Ivan on the shoulder.

Ivan turns.

Shifting from foot to foot,
the kennelman says guiltily:
We got a bit overzealous . . . strangled the boyar . . .

CLOSE-UP of Ivan's face.
At first at a loss.
Then stern and concentrated.
The "royal" look in his eyes.
And in his glance—approval.

I'll rule myself . . . without the boyars . . .

The kennelman looks apprehensively at Ivan.

I'll be a Tsar! . .

The eyes of Ivan gaze into the distance.

FADE OUT

THE CATHEDRAL
OF THE ASSUMPTION *

FADE IN
The frantic pealing of bells.

The coronation ceremony is taking place OFF SCREEN
Singing is heard.
But we cannot as yet see the ceremony itself.

* The *Uspensky Sobor*, a cathedral in the Kremlin.

The spectator sees pass before him various groups,
attentively gazing O F F   S C R E E N .

First we see, against a background of dark frescoes,
a group of indignant foreign ambassadors.

The foreigners grow heated:
Where has he suddenly sprung from—
this new—Moscow—Tsar?
The Prince of Muscovy has no right to style himself a Tsar!
The Pope won't recognize this as a coronation!
The Emperor will refuse to use the title in addressing him!
Europe will not recognize him as Tsar!

The voice of the Metropolitan, Pimen, speaking O F F   S C R E E N :
By our ancient title
I hereby crown with the royal crown
Grand Prince and Sovereign
Ivan son of Vasily . . .

Among the foreigners, prominently placed—a familiar figure:
it is the Humanist whom we saw with the Livonian embassy in an earlier
scene.
The old man is not very much older—only four years have gone by.
But now he himself is the Ambassador of Livonia.
And by his side is a young secretary.

Pimen's voice is heard:
And proclaim him, divinely crowned,
Tsar of Muscovy
and, of all great Rus,
Autocrat.

Kyrie Eleison!—comes ecstatically from the choir on the right.
Kyrie Eleison!—responds ecstatically the choir on the left.

The Humanist-Ambassador follows the ceremony intently
and whispers to himself:
That fledgling has flown a long way . . .

Kyrie Eleison!—the two choirs sing in unison.

While, beneath the ecstatic chorus,
against the background of dark frescoes, rays of sunshine lighting them,
the foreign ambassadors give rein to their indignation:
The Pope won't recognize this as a coronation!
The Emperor will refuse to use the title in addressing him!
Europe will not recognize him as Tsar!

And only the Humanist-Ambassador,
talking to himself, barely whispers, thin-lipped:
If he's strong—they'll recognize him . . .

One of the foreigners says to another:
Incidentally, certain of his own subjects too are not particularly
enthusiastic about this coronation . . .

And we see a group of boyars headed by the Staritskys.

The group is patently displeased;
Especially is this noticeable in the face of a tall, elderly woman.
The figure next to her is evidently her son—
he wears on his face an indifferent expression
and in his eyes a faraway look.

The one foreigner explains to the other:
It's not difficult to understand why these nobles are not pleased.
The one over there is a cousin of the Grand Prince—
Waldemar Staritsky—and next to him his mother.

His words are heard over a shot
of the Princess Euphrosyne Staritsky
with her son Vladimir.
And it is obvious that they are thinking what the ambassador is saying:
John's coronation as Tsar will hinder their path
to the throne of Muscovy!

A third foreigner intervenes in the conversation:
But there are also, it seems, partisans of John . . .

And his words sound over a group including the Zakharins and the
Glinskys.
Those are kinsfolk of the betrothed of the Grand Prince . . .
explains the first foreigner.

And we see Anastasia.
By the brightness of her attire and the silver of her ornaments

she gleams in the sunshine
amidst the kinsfolk surrounding her.
Her eyes sparkle with a joy more brilliant than the sun.

The Humanist-Ambassador of Livonia scathingly corrects
the first foreigner:
Not of the Grand Prince, but . . . of the Tsar!

The first foreigner snorts.
But the Livonian Ambassador reiterates:
Of the Tsar, now!

And at last we can see that now it has been concluded—the mystery
of anointment into Tsarship.

The venerable Metropolitan of Moscow, Pimen, completes the ritual.

In front of Pimen,
with his back to the spectator,
Ivan in the coronation mantle and full royal robes.
Around him—in billowing cloaks—
the bishops of the most important sees.

Pimen takes from a golden platter
the royal crown—the cap of Monomakh.
He gives it to Ivan to kiss.
He places it on Ivan's head.
He pronounces:
In the name of the Father, the Son and the Holy Ghost . . .

Ivan bows his head.

The words of Pimen:
Guard and preserve this crown!
Magnify it on the throne of truth,
fortify it with Thy might!
And subdue beneath Thy feet
every enemy and foe!

Ivan draws himself erect and turns round.

He is seventeen years old.

His mien is proud.
His eyes blaze.
Ivan stands rooted to the spot
while the invocation continues:

For Thine is the Kingdom,
the Power and the Glory,
in the name of the Father, the Son and the Holy Ghost . . .

Joyfully gazes Anastasia at Ivan.
Joyfully gaze the Glinskys and Zakharins.

. . . as it was in the beginning,
is now, and ever shall be,
world without end!

Gloomily the Staritskys frown.

Amen!—resoundingly sings the choir.

Ironically the foreigners watch.

Toward Ivan approach:
from the left—a young golden-haired prince,
from the right—an older black-browed boyar.

They take Ivan by the arms.
They lead him down the steps of the ambo before the altar.

Vessels filled with gold coins are brought to them.

And, raising high the vessels, in accordance with the ceremonial,
they pour over the young Tsar a golden shower.

The golden shower rings resoundingly.

Rings out the ecstatic
Kyrie Eleison!
of the Cathedral choir.
Rings out the joyous clamor of the bells.
Ring out the cries of greeting from the people. . . .

But, behold, the peal is silent.
The bells are stilled.

And soundlessly is spread before the feet of Ivan
a gold-embroidered carpet.

Stilled are the cries of the people.
All is stilled. . . .

And through the golden somnolence of the silent Cathedral
Ivan moves forward.

The retainers scarcely have time to unroll the carpet:
with such swift steps does Ivan advance towards them.

Like a young wild animal,
supple, shapely, sensuous,
he glides through the stillness up the eight steps
of the platform raised in the center—
"the prelatical ambo, denominated the theater."

In the rays of sunlight falling at the very center of the Cathedral he
stands still.

He is submerged in the vastness of the Cathedral.
He glitters in the half-darkness like an emerald:
reflections from the play of the sun waver like fire.

His eye flashes from the eminence like that of a young snow leopard.

Young.
Pale.
His gaze piercing.
Slightly asymmetrical of visage.
Black locks falling to his shoulders.

Like an icon in its frame the Tsar is encased in golden garments.

Within all is seething.
The bonds of his will bind him tighter than golden chains.

Р错 lu
Успенском Соборе

Holding himself back, he strives to speak quietly.
Holding himself back, he strives to speak evenly.

But thought surges after thought.
Word presses on word.
And in an unchecked, passionate flood
the speech of the youthful Tsar pours forth.

At first his tone is low.
Ivan speaks of power:
Now, for the first time a Prince of Muscovy
takes the crown of Tsar of all Rus
upon himself.

But, see, into his words he suddenly inserts
the first sparks of wrath
and in a fiery stream they flow with the flood of his speech—
Ivan recalls the rule of the boyars:

And thereby forever
boyar power over Rus—
multifarious,
crafty—
is put to an end.

The faces of the boyars darken.

He lifts his hand against the boyar power!—
mutters the Staritsky group.

With growing force
Ivan goes on angrily:
But to hold the Russian land
in a single hand
strength is needed.

Anastasia's eyes are fixed warmly on Ivan.
The young golden-haired prince is pleased.
The black-browed boyar is thoughtful.

And therefore henceforward we shall establish
an army—paid, trained,
permanent . . .

Boyar anger, like an ocean wave,
mounts at these words . . .

Ivan continues
in a voice that hints a threat:
He who, in the ranks of these Royal troops,
does not fight in person,
shall yet, in the great campaigns of the Tsar,
participate with money . . .

In explosive rejoinders, the boyars' anger
bursts forth at these words.

Euphrosyne mutters:
Risk your own money on your own head!

Ivan continues
calmly,
as though he did not notice this anger:
Likewise, also, the holy monasteries
with their great incomes
shall participate henceforward in our military enterprises.
The monasteries have amassed both treasure and territory
of which the Russian land has reaped no benefit . . .

A stir amongst the clergy.
The archimandrites are at a loss.
The archpresbyters are perplexed.
The Metropolitan is astounded.
The bishops are shaken.

Pimen, in surprise, drops his crosier.
The black-browed boyar catches it in its fall,
He hands it back to Pimen.

His eyes and Pimen's eyes have met.
So, evidently, have their thoughts.

The thoughts of the clergy and the boyars meet.
In counter to the Tsar, a wave of fury sweeps through the clergy
and fuses with the anger of the boyars.

Ivan sees the rising fury.
Ivan sees the growing wrath.
He sees the displeasure.

He continues still more forcefully:
*A strong power is needed
in order to crush
all who oppose the unity of Russian rule* . . .

From the Staritskys has come a muttering in answer.
Ivan's eyes have flashed toward the Staritskys.

Euphrosyne has sprung forward in a rage to answer.
The angry eyes of Euphrosyne are gleaming.
Vladimir holds his mother back.

The young golden-locked prince at the Tsar's right hand
gazes at him with enthusiasm.

On the Tsar's other side—the black-browed boyar
casts down his eyes, and his face darkens.

A murmur runs through the Cathedral.
An angry murmur of disapproval.

Only the foreigners look on detached, and derisive.
The issue appears not to concern them.
They are merely amused and mildly curious—
how will this discord between the young Tsar on the one hand,
and on the other the boyars and clergy,
work out in the end. . . .

Then, all of a sudden, the words of Ivan
have turned unexpectedly in their direction.

Quietly, barely audibly, Ivan continues:
. . . *For only a united realm*
strong,
welded within,
can likewise be firm without . . .

The foreigners have caught their breath.
The ambassadors are now on their guard.

Ivan continues, even more quietly.
And in his voice there seems to sound the distant echo of the song
that tells of the "Ocean-sea, Azure sea, Russian sea . . ."

And what does our fatherland now resemble
but a trunk,
severed at knee and elbow?
The upper reaches of our rivers—
the Volga, Dvina, Volkhov—
are beneath our rule,
but their outlets to the sea
are in alien hands . . .

Now still more clearly the Tsar's words seem to echo with the refrain
"Azure sea, Russian sea":
. . . *the maritime lands of our fathers and grandfathers—on the Baltic—*
have been rent from our soil . . .

The ambassadors have become worried.
Ivan sees their worry.

The ambassadors have become agitated.
Ivan sees their agitation.
And he proclaims, in loud and royal tones:
Therefore this day We crown Ourself
with dominion also over those lands, which now—temporarily—
lie beneath other sovereignties!

A fearful stir among the ambassadors.
The Livonian Ambassador raises his eyebrows:
A fledgling indeed!

A fledgling no longer—an eagle on the heights.

Like a mountain eagle, soaring above the storm,
So Ivan breasts the raging tide
of human breakers.

The song of the azure sea,
of the Russian sea,
rings high in the dome.

And, through the storm of wrath
of ambassadors,
boyars,
clergy—
tossed in the hurricane,
flung about in the whirlwind,
the medley of people,
passions,
songs,
fury—
Ivan hurls in conclusion:
Two Romes fell
but the third—
Moscow—
shall stand,
and a fourth shall never be!
And in that Third Rome—
as ruler of Muscovy—
as sole Master
from this day forth shall I reign
ALONE!

And with these words he suddenly breaks off.

Rising above the hurricane of passions,
the deacon chants:
> *To the Grand Prince of Muscovy,*
> *I-o-a-nnis son of Vasily,*
> *Tsar and Autocrat of all Russia—*
> *Long life!*

The storm in the Cathedral sweeps to a tempest.
People are cast about in raging confusion.

56

In the midst of the storm, pale, his eyes burning,
like a rock—
alone—
stands Ivan.

The choir ecstatically takes up:
Long life!
Long life!

The joy of the Glinskys and Zakharins,
The rage of the Staritskys,
The wrath of the ambassadors
and the church chanting
blend in a general din.
The Cathedral hums like a beehive.

Long life!
Long life!

Euphrosyne Staritsky hisses: .
The wedding's fixed for tomorrow.
We'll celebrate this "Master's" wedding!
The Staritskys bunch together in a tighter huddle.

The chanting surges.
The bells clamor.

The foreigners:
The Pope won't permit it!
The Emperor won't agree to it!
Europe'll never recognize it!

The Livonian Ambassador says:
If he's strong—everyone'll recognize it!
And adds, to his secretary:
He mustn't be strong . . .

And while the rest grow heated,
the old diplomat says with a sigh:
The time has come to undo the purse strings . . .

And during this time when through the Cathedral rise
the Church-Slavonic chants
and the clamor of the bells,
the old diplomat and the young secretary
begin closely to scrutinize the entourage of Ivan:
on whom shall they place their stake?

THE CAMERA HALTS at the young prince on Ivan's right.
The young prince is gazing rapturously at Ivan.

And, unexpectedly, it is of him that the Ambassador speaks:
That one!

The secretary is astonished:
But he's the first man after Ivan.
The first friend of Ivan and the second man in the State!

But the Ambassador answers deliberately:
Ambition is more terrible than greed . . .
No man can be satisfied while he is first . . .
after another . . .

The young secretary is not convinced:
But he has everything!
He needs nothing!

Yet again the old man speaks:
No man knows the limits of human desire . . .
And his glance turns to the other side of the young prince.
There, too, has looked the secretary.

And we see that the young prince
has changed the direction of his gaze from Ivan to Anastasia.
And his look has grown sullen.

The Livonian Ambassador glances ironically at his secretary.
The secretary apologetically lowers his head.
And the old diplomat says, in businesslike style:
Occupy yourself with Prince Andrew Kurbsky.

And, beneath the incessant clangor of the bells, we see
the musing face of young Prince Kurbsky.
He is gazing at Anastasia.
And, from the expression on his face, we come to believe
that the Ambassador was not, maybe, quite so far wrong . . .

Long life!
Long life!—
clamors the choir.

FADE OUT

HEADFALL RING*

The frantic clamor of the bells merges
into a loud roaring of crowds.
The glittering interior of the Cathedral changes
to the dark streets of Moscow.
The streets are seething with people.
The roar rolls along with the hurrying crowds.

Staritsky kinsmen are scattered in the crowd.
They are stirring up the people.
They are urging the people to listen to a voice from Headfall Ring,
and pay heed.

The people listen.
Listening—two brothers: Foma and Yeroma Chokhov.

The Tsar is bewitched!—
comes the voice from Headfall Ring:
Bewitched by the kin of the future Tsarina!
Bewitched by the Glinskys!

And we see the tall figure of an idiot beggar,
raving,
with foam on his lips,
crying out a message to the people—
calling on them to save the young Tsar from the spells of the Evil Ones:

* *Lobnoye Mesto*, a circular stone platform outside the Kremlin on the square now
called Red Square, used in medieval times as a place of execution.

He turns from his own kin, the Staritskys.
He oppresses his faithful boyars.
He lays hands upon the treasures of the monasteries and of the church!

Nikola the Simple cries, with foam on his lips:
For these offenses the Lord God will send down great woes upon the
people!
Fire will come down from heaven!

And shouts rise above the crowd in response:
Down with the Glinskys!—cries Foma.
And it is patent that his cry is prompted by exclamations
cunningly flung out by partisans of the Staritskys.

The most excited of all among the crowd
is a stalwart ginger-haired lad named Gregory.

The din floats above the night square.
Torches flare.
Bells clang.

To the bell ringers on the belfry there climbs up
one of the retinue of the Staritsky group.
Together with him are the bondsmen Kozma and Demyan.
These latter conceal themselves at one side.

Down with the Glinskys!—
Everyone is shouting insistently.

The din floats above the night square.
The din merges with the clanging of the bells.
The black night-square seethes.

THE HALL OF GOLD

It is far from the square to the apartments of the Tsar.
The clangor reaches from far off to the nuptial hall.
It merges

With the shouts:
Bitter! Bitter!*

And, enveloped in the shouts of the revelers,
the Tsar,
from the lips of the Tsarina,
completing his kiss, breaks away . . .

Anastasia blushes.
The Tsar is delighted.
The guests shout.
The clangor is heard from far off.

* The cry "Bitter! Bitter!" by guests at Russian weddings is, by ancient custom, an in-
junction to the bridegroom to kiss the bride. The implication: "Sweeten things up
a bit!"

The Tsar hears the pealing of the bells:
Why does Moscow
ring so resoundingly?

And, from her high place of nuptial godmother, to the Tsar
Euphrosyne Staritsky flatteringly replies:
The joy of the people of Moscow is flowing over . . .

With Pimen, who occupies a place of honor,
Staritsky exchanges glances.

Above Moscow—
the frantic pealing of the bells.

The old Glinsky witch—the Tsar's grandmother—practices sorcery!—
Nikola "Big-Fool," the simpleton, is at it as strongly as ever:
She tears the hearts out of human beings.
She sprinkles houses with human blood.
And, from that blood, fire is born—
houses burn!

Gripped by the speech, Gregory shouts:
Burn the Glinskys themselves!

And the Staritsky partisans piercingly take up the cry:
Cross over the river*—and burn the Glinskys!

The din floats above the square.
The din merges with the pealing of the bells.

The black night-square seethes . . .

In the nuptial Hall of Gold,
Ivan turns to Kurbsky and Kolychev with a question:
Why are my closest friends sad at this moment?

Kurbsky answers evasively:
Well, Sovereign-Tsar,

* The actual cry was "To Zamoskvorechiye"—the suburb of old Moscow on the other
side of the river.

there is an apt saying among the people:
"when marriage begins—friendship ends . . ."

Anastasia has turned toward Kurbsky.
Kurbsky has averted his glance.

Ivan laughs.
He turns to his other friend:
And what does Fyodor Kolychev answer?

Kolychev rises.
He bows to the Tsar.
Speaks:
Thou art breaking, Tsar, with the ancient customs;
great discord will arise therefrom . . .

And, as though underlining the words of Kolychev,
pouring like a tempestuous sea,
from the far square of Headfall Ring
the crowds of people surge forward.
Cries resound:
To the Tsar!

It is far from the square to the apartments of the Tsar—
the cry does not carry to the Tsar's apartments.

Kolychev continues:
Against the Tsar I dare not go.
With thee I cannot go . . .
He says, with a bow:
Permit me to retire to a monastery . . .

From her place of honor Euphrosyne
is listening to the distant hubbub with malicious joy.

Ivan is hurt.
He replies to Kolychev:
Thou wouldst change the earthly Tsar for the Tsar of Heaven?
Well, betwixt thee and the Tsar of Heaven
I shall not stand.
He waves his hand:

Go!
Pray for us—sinners . . .
With sorrow he looks into the eyes of Kolychev.
And speaks, deeply moved:
One thing only I ask:
When an ill time comes do not desert me—
in the hour of need return at our summons . . .

Fyodor Kolychev bows low to the Tsar . . .

A servitor approaches Euphrosyne—
as though to pour wine—
and whispers close in her ear—
disturbing news.
The eyes of Euphrosyne sparkle with pleasure.

Somewhere, far off, the clamor of bells is now a tocsin.
Somewhere, far off, the vague din is coming nearer.
It is heard through the wedding music.

The din is more audible.
Someone
who is near the windows
begins to listen to the far-off din.

The gaze of the Tsar is fixed on Anastasia—
he hears nothing . . .

Kolychev goes up to the Metropolitan Pimen.
The Metropolitan looks at the boyar with sympathy.
He blesses the boyar.
Speaks:
Go to Solovyets Monastery.
I ordain you abbot . . .

The roar is louder . . .
And, in order to drown the roar,
Euphrosyne gives a sign with her kerchief.

A wedding song rings out:

In and round the city the Tsar wanders,
Wanders, seeking for a bride,
Into the attics of houses peering,
Looking for a white, white swan. . . .

Outside the windows, the hubbub is growing louder.
Euphrosyne gives a second sign—
the song thunders more resoundingly.
    Open, gates,
    Open wide . . .
The doors swing open
The hubbub and the song are both drowned in cries of rejoicing—
down the wide staircase float dishes:
roast swans held aloft,
white swans
decorated with silver tiaras.
Beneath the cries is heard the song:
    The white swan swims,
    Plump-white,
    Desire-white,
    Crowned with light!
The chorus is sung a second time in honor of the Tsarina:
    Desire-white,
    Crowned with light!

And against the background of this general rejoicing,
triumphantly,
a cup in her hands,
rises from the table
she who is to say the wedding benediction—
Euphrosyne.

The dishes with the swans float by.
The white swans float by the Tsarina.
Their silver tiaras gleam . . .

Euphrosyne pronounces,
in a loud voice
drowning all and everything:
A health to thee,
Tsar Ivan son of Vasily!
And a flourishing future

to thy works!
Glory!

Every cup has been raised.
The cups are carried to the lips.
The Tsar is glorified with wine.

All cry: *Glory!*

First to drain his cup is the Tsar's closest friend—
Kurbsky.
High he lifts his empty cup—in accordance with custom.
He has swung his arm:
Heigh— . . .
His glance has lighted on Anastasia.
His brow has darkened.
In accordance with custom he has smashed his cup to pieces on the floor.
. . . *—ho!"*

Only, just a little more strongly than prescribed by custom,
as though in anger,
as though consumed with jealousy.

Euphrosyne has smiled, a smile of irony, of understanding.
Among the others, none has noticed . . .

All lift their empty cups.
They are ready to hurl them to the ground—
in accordance with custom.

They have swung their arms:
Heigh— . . .
A deafening crash bursts.
Not of cups, smashing on the ground,
but of windows, smashed into bits by stones!

The pealing tocsin bursts through the broken windows.
The din of the crowd fills the hall with cries.
Through the broken windows the wind blows, howling,
snuffing out, in one breath, a hundred candles . . .

The hall is plunged in darkness.

And, through that darkness, in ominous scarlet tongues,
creeps the distant glow of a fire . . .

The guests have rushed to the windows.
Outside the windows is a conflagration:
Across the river—the houses burn!

In the courtyard murmur the angry people.
Outside the windows rage the flames.

Above the raging fire looms the bell tower.
The Staritskys' minions cast down the bells from the belfries.

The Staritskys' bondsman—
Demyan—
cuts the bell ropes with a knife.

Actively helping Demyan
is Nikola "Big-Fool," the Simpleton.
By all appearances, he is far from simple.

Below, into the flames plunges a bell—
the biggest—the "Harbinger of Blessings."
After it small bells rattle down like peas.

Through the broken windows the boyars watch the fire.

In the vast festive hall of the Tsar
only two are left together in the gloom:

the white dove—Anastasia;
by one unextinguished candle,
the last,
she is pallidly lit.

And Ivan, in the rays of the bloody glow,
towering like an angry giant.

You would rouse the people against me,
boyars!
Not peace but a sword you have asked for . . .

He draws himself up—
the shadow flits across the vaulted ceiling like a black phantom.
Fixedly the Tsar drinks in the glow with his eyes:
And the sword you shall get!

With a roar and a clatter the doors are flung open—
into the hall burst the people.

They light the hall with long torches.

They press against the guard.
They jostle.
They trample.

Kurbsky and Kolychev rush to the rescue of Ivan.
They wish to defend the Tsar from the people.

But Ivan orders:
Let the people pass!

The guards of the Tsar do not hearken—
with a forest of halberds they halt the people.

Angered, the people force back the guard.
Foremost of all—the ginger lad Gregory.

The tumult spreads.

Ivan throws himself forward to part the tumult.
At that moment, with a titanic wrench,
Gregory forces his way through the guard.

Having raised a club above his head with a titanic swing,
he hurls himself at Ivan.

With a cry Anastasia closes her eyes.
The club must surely crush Ivan . . .

But, at the last moment,
just in time, beneath it jumps
Kurbsky.

He covers Ivan with his body—
warding off the blow to one side.

Kolychev seizes Gregory.
Forces him to his knees before the Tsar.

Kurbsky and Kolychev glare fiercely at Gregory . . .

The guard swept aside, the people in their rush stand rooted.
They recognize the Tsar.
They fall on their knees before the Tsar.

Great Sovereign,
we come to make plaint against the Glinskys!
We ask justice!
The Glinskys have been practicing sorcery.

Foma Chokhov exclaims:
Dread omens threaten Moscow . . .

Yeroma Chokhov exclaims:
The bells fall by themselves from the belfries!

And, rising from their knees,
the people cry,
Yield, Tsar, to the sign from God!

Foremost of all, more than any other,
rages the ginger lad Gregory.

Not far behind are the Brothers Chokhov:
Foma and Yeroma.
The crowd seethes.

Tsar Ivan gazes long at the people.
He is separated from the people by his friends—
Kurbsky and Kolychev.

It is the first encounter of Ivan and the people
face to face.

With an imperious gesture Ivan parts the guard
standing between him and the common people.
He thrusts aside Kurbsky, clears out of the way Kolychev.
He approaches the excited giant—Gregory.

The people grow still.
Kurbsky has assumed a position to protect Anastasia.

IVAN:
Magic, you say? Bells have fallen?
He stretches out his hand:
Any head that believes in magic is, like a bell . . .
He taps his finger on the forehead of Gregory:
. . . empty.

Titters in the crowd.

IVAN:
Can a head fly off by itself?

There is already laughter in the crowd.
Gregory is flummoxed.

Ivan says gently:
To fly off—it must be cut off.
He has drawn his finger along Gregory's neck.
And then his eyes have given such a look
that cold sweat has broken out on Gregory's skin.
Something of the future "Terrible" blazed in that look
of the young Ivan.

But Ivan continues lightly:
With bells is it likewise.
Indeed, whosoever without the Tsar's permission has cut down a bell
shall speedily, by the Tsar's decree, have his head cut also.

The Tsar's speech pleases the people.
The Brothers Chokhov like the Tsar.

FOMA:
This Tsar fellow, it's plain, has a noddle on him!
YEROMA:
His eyes see right down to the root of things!

The people laugh approvingly.

After a pause, Gregory himself unexpectedly bursts into a loud guffaw,
having felt that the storm has passed over.

However, in the depths of the hall, Vladimir Staritsky
fearfully passes his hand over his own neck . . .
He has caught the stern glance of his mother on him.
He has felt embarrassed—hid his hand in his long sleeve.

The Staritskys' bondsman—Demyan—looks fearfully at Ivan . . .

Ivan speaks with heat to the people:
And We shall cut off heads ruthlessly!
Stamp out treason.
Tear out boyar treachery by the roots!

The crowd is pleased with the Tsar's speech.
The people exclaim approvingly.

Like one spellbound,
at the Tsar gazes
Anastasia.
In her excitement she involuntarily clutches at Kurbsky's hand.

Kurbsky presses her hand responsively.

Anastasia has looked round.
She has caught his glance fixed on her.
She has taken away her hand.
And curtly said:
Of that, Prince, you must not even dare think!
I stand devoted to a great service—
of the Tsar of Muscovy I am the loyal slave!

73

She has strained toward Ivan.
She looks at him in ecstasy.

Kurbsky's brow has darkened.
He bites his moustaches angrily.

And, some distance away, Ivan is speaking to the people.
He does not shout.
Nor grow heated.
Judiciously, commonsensically,
gradually
he speaks on to them:
Our lands are great and bountiful,
but of order there is little in them.
We shall not call in mercenaries.
We shall introduce order ourselves.
We shall stamp out sedition.
Working people, tradesmen, merchants—
We shall not let be harmed . . .

So Ivan has spoken to his people in council,
to the many-headed council . . .

The people hearken to the Tsar attentively.
Near the Tsar's feet
they seat themselves on the ground.

Not this did the Staritsky woman expect,
not this did she plan.

Up to the Staritsky woman runs
her bondsman Demyan;
excitedly he exclaims:
Three emissaries from Kazan to the Tsar . . .

A flash lights the eyes of the old woman:
Let them in!—she bids.

Interrupting the Tsar's speech,
Insolently and noisily enter the three Kazan envoys.

74

The people turn toward the envoys.

The chief envoy speaks, without bowing to the Tsar:
Kazan breaks friendship with Moscow.
Alliance with Moscow ends.
War with Moscow starts!

The crowd has jumped up as one man.
Slowly Ivan has stood erect.
He has straightened his shoulders.

The envoy continues:
Kazan—big.
Moscow—small.

The second envoy clarifies:
KICHKINE . . .

The first says:
Moscow—finish.
The Great Khan . . .

The envoys bow.

. . . *sends a knife.*
Russian Tsar not wish have shame:
Then Russian Tsar end himself.

The third envoy shouts:
KUTARDY!

The first envoy holds out to Ivan
a rusty dagger.

But here too takes place that
which the Staritskys did not expect.

The people raise their staves with cries of wrath.

Ivan leaps to the envoy.

He grasps the rusty dagger.
He cries hotly:
God sees—We do not seek warfare.
But the time has passed when the usurper might dictate
to the Moscow Tsar.
And this dagger shall pierce those who have raised their hand against
                                            Muscovy!

He has shouted:
We shall finish with Kazan forever . . .
He has turned the dagger point against the envoy:
It is We who shall launch the campaign—against Kazan!

To Kazan!—
the call has been taken up with enthusiasm first by Gregory.
*To Kazan!—*the call has been taken up with enthusiasm by the people.

That same cry comes from the courtyard.
It bursts through the broken windows.

To Kazan!

Beneath the windows,
on the courtyard,
the people clamor.

Ivan, stirred and flushed with triumph,
looks round for Anastasia.

She, radiant with happiness,
is led to Ivan by Kurbsky.

Ivan embraces Kurbsky.
He proclaims:
I appoint you to lead the vanguard!

Kurbsky is proud.
He looks around grandly.

The three envoys stand in confusion.

Yet louder ring the cries:
To Kazan!
The music swells.
The crowd is in general movement.

Gregory rakes into his mighty embrace
the chief Kazan envoy.

The people run along passageways to the high staircase.
High above the people,
Gregory lifts the Kazan envoy,
and, from the high staircase, hurls him
down
into the crowd below.

Yet louder and in unison
the cry is heard:
To Kazan!

The long-drawn-out cry is changed into a song:
  Forge the copper cannon true,
    cannoneers,
  And trusty arquebuses too,
    cannoneers . . .
Pikes and axes being forged.

Foma and Yeroma are busy forging.
  There'll be sisters to the cannon,
    cannoneers,
  Pikes and sabers sharp,
    cannoneers.
Cannon being cast.

The long-drawn-out singing rises:
  Straight is the way,
    'cross the Tartar steppe.
  Famed City of Kazan—
    comes woe, bitter woe.

To the sound of the singing,
out of the fire,
cannon being born.
New.
Huge . . .

A *fine cannon!*—the voice of Ivan is heard suddenly.
But what is it called?

Bully Boy!—quietly answers the chief gunsmith.
"Bully Boy" let it be! gaily says Ivan.
The remaining guns,
all old friends,
under the measured beat of the hammers,
are christened in turn:
Lion!
Wolf!
Singer!
Basilisk!
Bully Boy!—cries Foma.
The singing rings yet more heartily:

> *Lay true the cannon of the Tsar,*
> > *cannoneers . . .*
> *Move the siege towers to the wall,*
> > *cannoneers . . .*

Foma forging axes.

Yeroma casting cannon.

The song goes on.

> *Against Kazan's wall,*
> > *cannoneers . . .*
> *Good Muscovy lads all,*
> > *cannoneers . . .*

Cannon being cast.
YEROMA:
The lads are doing a good job . . .

Halberds being forged.
FOMA:
Wonderful fellows.

> *Straight is the way,*
> *'cross the Tartar steppe.*
> *Famed city of Kazan—*
> *'Tis hard, heavy toil* . . .

Guns being dragged along mushy roads.
Immense and unwieldy guns.

Muscles are straining,
ropes are being hauled—
the cannon "Basilisk" is being drawn by
twenty-five sweating horses . . .

Royal troops* march forward.
A forest of axes passes into the darkness.

Soon it is quite dark.
In the darkness some kind of movement is vaguely perceptible.
We hear the scraping sound of spades
and the heavy blows of pickaxes.

From the orchestra comes the sound of the gunners' song.
And heavily, in rhythm, strike the pickaxes . . .

KAZAN

Gradually, from the darkness, emerge the outlines of separate figures.
Spades, picks, and mattocks are being strenuously plied.
Among those digging, directing the labor, is a tall, sturdy lad.
He is the foreman.

* *Streltsi*—literally "sharpshooters"; first they were arquebusiers, later musketeers. Established by Ivan as the first State standing army, in contrast to levies supplied by nobles as a feudal duty.

Somewhere the work has bogged down.
The foreman has seized a pick from someone
and himself turned to the job.
The soil is excavated furiously.

The black earth is removed on sledges.
Simultaneously with the sledges, there emerges at the exit from the mine
the sturdy lad.
It is Gregory.
He is black with dirt, sweating and hot,
but keen and eager.

Gregory crawls out of the pit.
He blinks in the light, like a ginger cat.
He opens his eyes wide.

In front of him, above the pit, stands Tsar Ivan.
Beside Ivan is Kurbsky.
And a foreigner—Engineer Rasmussen.
High personages.

Behind the Tsar—the endless Tartar steppe.

Voices ring out in song:
Oh, woe, bitter woe,
thou Tartar steppe.
The Tsar's mail gleams against the coming dawn.
On his breast burns a golden sun.

The armor worn by Kurbsky shines silver,
bright.
Hard work,
Tsar's work . . .

Gregory reports:
The mine can now be packed with gunpowder.

Ivan is pleased:
We have waited a month.

Enough of waiting.
Long since time for the assault!

And we see, in the first light
of the approaching dawn,
that in front of us is not only the mine,
but the whole Russian camp, on the hilly side of the river.

Above the entrenchments stand cannon.

In the trenches are Royal troops;
two or three of the men we recognize as having been among those
who burst into the Tsar's hall.

On the other side of the river—in the foggy mist—
looms the outline
of besieged Kazan.
It grows lighter.
The fort of Kazan is still clad in morning mist.

Kurbsky causes Tartar prisoners to be led out above the entrenchments.
He has them tied, half naked, to palings in full view of the city.
Through interpreters, Kurbsky bids them shout
to the defenders of Kazan a proposal to surrender:
Cry: "Kazan, surrender!"

One, despairing, calls out
in Tartar.
One has lowered his gaze sullenly to the ground.
One is forced to cry out
in Tartar.

The cry carries to the walls of Kazan.
Several heads appear.
They listen.
Suddenly, above the walls, rises the figure of a tall old man
in a white turban.
By his side are some young princes—Tartar commanders.

And the old man in the turban shouts from the height of the Kazan
                                                 citadel

to the bound Tartar prisoners:
Better you perish at our hands
than die
by those of uncircumcised giaours!

A flight of arrows has whistled from the walls of Kazan—
the dead prisoners droop from the palings.

Kurbsky spitefully waves his hand:
If they won't—now they needn't.

Kurbsky's signal has been caught,
And passed on.

Barrels of gunpowder are rolling into the mine.
The barrels roll with a rumble.

And as they rumble Ivan in a rage hastens
to Kurbsky, standing on the entrenchments.

Angrily Ivan upbraids Kurbsky
for purposeless cruelty:
Senseless savagery—stupidity.
Even an untaught beast when it bites has a purpose!

Kurbsky is stung to the quick. He boils up. Loses control of himself.
He grasps Ivan round the waist.
Ivan is astounded at the audacity of Kurbsky.

Gregory has run up with a report.
He sees what is happening.
He stands amazed.

Ivan strongly gripped by Kurbsky.
Kurbsky has realized that he has gone too far.

Between them as they quarrel there flies past an arrow.
Two more have stuck in the paling.

Quick as lightning Kurbsky presses Ivan to the paling.
Gregory is ready to hurl himself on Kurbsky.

But Kurbsky explains to Ivan that he was trying
to cover him from the arrow:
I sought to protect thee from the arrow . . .

Gregory glares furiously at Kurbsky.

The underground rumble of the rolling barrels grows louder.

Ivan says to Kurbsky:
If from the arrow . . . then thanks.
With a wave of the hand he dismisses him to the vanguard.

With hatred in his eyes Gregory glares after Kurbsky.

Kurbsky mounts his horse.
He speaks to himself:
The Livonian was right—he always treats me like a puppy.

Ivan catches Gregory's look at Kurbsky.
He sends Gregory back into the mine.
He himself gazes after his friend.

Kurbsky, mounted on a white horse,
is lost in the ranks of his troops.

Slowly, thoughtfully, Ivan says:
Some arrows fly timefully . . .

Alongside Ivan, a voice
as though speaking his thought aloud:
Worse than Tartar arrows
is boyar hatred . . .

The Tsar has turned round.
Before him, the chief gunner
speaks deliberately:
Not arrows—but boyar princes—
need fearing.

Your name?—Ivan casts his gaze upon him.

Alexey Basmanov—
the man says—*Daniel's son.*

A smile of approval
passes across the Tsar's face:
The name of a boyar-hater
shall not slip my memory . . .

He has turned.
He has gone off toward his tent.

Basmanov speaks
to a young lad—his lieutenant:
See there, Fyodor!
See, son—
the Tsar of all Russia . . .

The Tsar . . .
repeats Fyodor
in awe.

He looks after Ivan, without blinking.
He stares open-eyed.
He does not remove his eyes from the Tsar.

Ivan high up, in front of the tents,
above Kazan,

is silhouetted against the morning sky.

Gregory in the mine is surrounded by barrels of gunpowder.
The Brothers Chokhov, Foma and Yeroma, are there too.
Other gunners assisting, they stand a candle in the midst of the barrels.

To the base of the candle
Gregory fastens the fuses.

For the first time in their lives Foma and Yeroma are silent—
the importance of the moment overcomes them . . .

A similar candle,
where everyone can see it,
is put on the ground above
by the foreigner—Engineer Rasmussen.

The candle underground burns.
The candle on the surface burns.
Ivan looks at Kazan.
Kurbsky looks, stationed at the head of his troops.
The gunners watch . . .

The candle burns slowly.
Its flame wavers slightly in the wind.

The Royal troops are watching. Yeroma is watching.
Silence all round.
On the walls, the Tartars are watching.

Slowly the candle burns.

C L O S E - U P—Ivan by his tent.

C L O S E - U P—the flame.

C L O S E - U P—Kurbsky.

C L O S E - U P—the candle.

Already the candle is half burned down.

The giant Gregory, oil-smothered, dirty, breathes heavily—
tensely.

Nervously the flame wavers.

Another quarter of the candle is gone.
The Tsar watches, motionless as a statue.

The priests are dumb before their icons.

Kurbsky gnaws his moustache.

The flame starts guttering at the end of the candle.

Gregory's eyes are screwed up.

The candle has completely burned away.

Silence.
The Tsar holds his breath.

Kurbsky is taut.

The guns are motionless.

But no explosion comes . . .

The Tsar shouts:
What then has become of your underground thunders?

Gregory dashes off.
He runs to the mine.
The foreign engineer Rasmussen grabs him by the scruff.
He does not let him go.
He holds him by the arms.

Kurbsky has sent a derisive look at the Tsar.
The Tsar has drawn his brows together:
The gunners hither!

The gunners fling themselves down at the Tsar's feet.

The gunners have been dragged to the gallows.
The gunner's tunics have been torn off.
They have been left in their shirts.

Nooses have been laid round their necks.

87

Candles have been placed in their hands.

Gregory has wrenched himself away from Rasmussen.
He has thrown himself on his knees before the Tsar:
This is not treachery, Sovereign—
a candle burns faster in the open air;
underground it goes more gently.

The Tsar does not listen to him.
He bids the gunners be strung up.

Gregory hurls himself toward the gunners.
With his own hands he dons a noose.
Holy Cross!—
he bows.
Lord!—
he sinks to his knees.

The ropes are slowly hoisted over the gallows.

Underground, in the darkness, the candle has burned right down to the
                                                                  fuses.
The fire runs along the fuses.

Gregory raises his head.
The ropes have been drawn tight over the gallows.

An explosion has gone off—
the wall has staggered.

A second explosion—
the Kazan tower is crumbling.

A third explosion.

Gregory comes running up to the Tsar, just as he was, the noose round
                                                                  his neck.

Fifty rubles for the gunners!—
shouts Ivan, exalted.

Kurbsky has rushed forward to the assault.

The song has thundered:
> *The black powder's vomited,*
> > *cannoneers,*
> *The horsemen have charged,*
> > *cannoneers . . .*

The troops have leaped forward through the breach:
> *The crows have flown on,*
> > *cannoneers,*
> *The Warriors' prayers are said,*
> > *cannoneers . . .*

Not a shot greets them.
It is as though no one were left alive.

The siege ladders have surged forward.
Kurbsky in front.

Ivan turns away.
He cannot control himself—
he fears for his friend.
He hides his face in the folds of his tent.

Quite suddenly Kazan has burst forth
with a shower of arrows, of stones,
with a hail of burning pitch . . .
> *Ah! Woe, bitter woe;*
> > *thou Tartar steppe . . .*

Every third man in the ranks has fallen . . .
> *Hard work,*
> > *Tsar's work . . .*

Ivan has turned round.
Kurbsky is unharmed—
his armor glitters in the sun.

Ivan has given a signal:
To the aid of Kurbsky!

The cannon crash.

Ivan calls off
the pet names:
Lion!
Wolf!
Singer!
Bully Boy!
The cannon crash out in sequence.
They crash out together.

And behold, Kurbsky is already upon the walls—
he has been the first to reach them.

He waves aloft the standard.
On the wall, through the smoke,
like a bright dot,
shines his armor.

Ivan towers above the cannon:
Now indeed I'll be Tsar;
the Tsar of Muscovy shall be recognized everywhere!

The thunder of cannon,
bells,
fanfare,
music,
ring out in reply to the Tsar's pronouncement.

We see rise up the domes,
hard by Headfall Ring,
of the Cathedral of St. Basil the Blessed.
And in an endless procession the embassies flow forward
to glorify the Moscow Tsar.
They come to stand within the shadow of the Tsar of Muscovy.

An Astrakhan embassy.
A Cherkassian embassy.
Gifts sent from Siberia.

The herald proclaims their names
as they step into the Tsar's courtyard.

In the courtyard
are a lion and a lioness—
To the glorious Tsar of Muscovy,
from his sister,
a gift from England's Queen . . .

THE PALACE CORRIDORS

Into the clamor of the music there gradually blends
a melancholy bell.

And already the people stand silent by the Tsar's apartments.
On the staircases and in the corridors.
Rasmussen, distressed, stands with bended knee.
Nearby stands Vyrodkov.

The boyars stand silent in the hallways.

Beneath an arch, saddened, the merchant Stroganovs.

And some distance away, at the bottom of the stairs,
in the dark habit of a soldier—
the warrior-captain Alexey Basmanov.

In the Audience Chamber—the ambassadors.
Here mingle West and East:
England and Persia,
Siberia and Italy.

The foreigners whisper:
How fares the Tsar?
How is the health of the Tsar of Muscovy?
The Tsar is sick.

The word "Tsar" is pronounced by all with notable respect
and deference.

A young foreigner is explaining to someone:
While on the very way back from Kazan, the Tsar fell ill.

The Livonian Ambassador remarks sarcastically to him:
So even for you he has now started to be Tsar?

Piqued, the foreigner turns away.

A group of boyars. A little to one side—Kurbsky.
Among the boyars—Euphrosyne Staritsky.
With a sigh she says:
Just is the Lord,
Who raiseth on high above other princes the Prince of Muscovy,
And bringeth him also to the dust . . .

Pondering stands Kurbsky.
A voice beside him:
Well, Prince, always second? . . .
Kurbsky has turned around.

In front of him—Euphrosyne Staritsky.
She laughs soundlessly.

Thou didst love Anastasia
Ivan took her.
Thou didst win Kazan in battle—
yet Ivan is the victor.
To him the glory,
while to thee . . .
she venomously emphasizes:
. . . for service to the State
they'll cut thee off a tiny bit of land . . .
Abruptly altering her tone, she speaks swiftly:
Thou didst capture Kazan for Ivan
to the injury of the boyars,
on thine own head be it . . .

Kurbsky in displeasure has turned away.
But, OFF SCREEN, sounds the voice of Euphrosyne:
And that head of thine is not long for thy shoulders . . .
Kurbsky has suddenly become alert.

With emphasis Euphrosyne continues:
Not quickly will the Tsar forget the Kazan arrow . . .

Kurbsky has abruptly flamed with rage.

Euphrosyne has gripped him by the arm and,
staring him straight in the eye, says:
And should he forget . . . there'll always be someone to remind him!
Suddenly both start, and glance aside:

beside them on the staircase there has slowly passed
the shadow of Malyuta (of Gregory Skuratov-Byelsky).

Euphrosyne whispers in the ear of Kurbsky:
With Ivan living Kurbsky cannot live . . .

Malyuta has disappeared from view.

But God is merciful!—
Euphrosyne has added, pointing to the procession
that is entering the inner chamber of the Tsar.

At its head is the Metropolitan Pimen bearing the holy sacraments.
Behind him the black habit of a monk is borne
by seven priests.*
Then monks with lighted candles.

A clerk explains to the foreigners:
They come to give extreme unction to the Tsar . . .
One foreigner says to another foreigner:
It is a custom in this land just before death . . .

Dolefully tolls a single bell.
The monks sing the 51st Psalm:
    Have mercy upon me, O God!
The procession has disappeared into the inner apartments.
From afar is borne the prayer:
Once more, once more, pray for peace unto the Lord.

* It was a tradition for Russian princes to abdicate temporal power, renounce the world
and become monks immediately before death, that they might die in the odor of
sanctity.

All is subdued:
the door has closed.
Complete silence.

Dolefully tolls the single bell.

Alone, amidst the luxury, all in darkness, sorrowing
stands Basmanov.

Euphrosyne has sternly questioned Kurbsky:
To whom wilt thou kiss the cross in fealty?

Kurbsky is astonished:
To the son of Ivan—his heir Dmitry . . .

And Anastasia?—
Euphrosyne breaks in:
Thy ambition is to play Telepnev to the widow?

Kurbsky has turned away offended.

Beware, Prince, don't hazard too highly!—

and, after a pause, she has added:
Kiss the cross to my son Vladimir!

Kurbsky looks at her questioningly,
then transfers his glance across the chamber.

In a corner sits Vladimir Staritsky.
In apparently profound bliss he is catching flies.
Not figuratively—
but in actual fact.
Only, by no means can he catch them:
he always grabs air.

Kurbsky transfers his mocking gaze
away from him and back to Euphrosyne.

Euphrosyne has grasped his thought.
She has spoken out crudely:
That's exactly why! . . .

She has added hotly:
Men like thee gold cannot buy.
To such as thee a kingdom must be given.
With Vladimir enthroned, thou'lt hold
                    Moscow's reins . . .

More aggrieved than regretful, she has continued:
He is worse than a baby.
His mind is afflicted . . .

Vladimir has reached after a fly.
And again grabbed at air.

Euphrosyne has finished:
Complete master thou'dst be! . . .

In the bedchamber of Ivan
the unction pursues its course.
Pimen takes a Gospel,
opens it, straightens it out and
"lays its written pages upon the head of the ailing,
as though it were the hand of the Savior himself,
healing the sick by touch."

The face of Ivan, part covered by the Gospel.
The Gospel is held by the seven priests.
In their free hands burn seven candles.

The pallid lips of Ivan
ceaselessly mutter beneath the Gospel:
Lord, have mercy . . .
Lord, have mercy . . .
Lord, have mercy . . .
His hands are lain crosswise upon his breast.

In chorus the seven ecclesiastics chant . . .

Anastasia weeps.

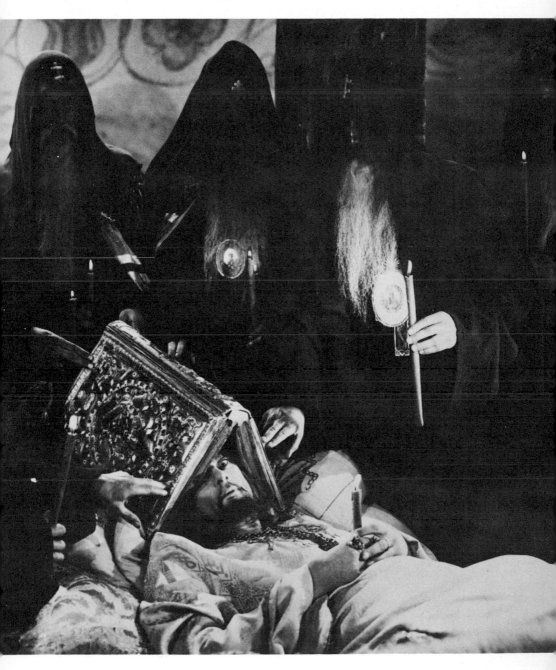

In the depths of the chamber outside, Vladimir Staritsky is still trying
to catch flies.
And always missing.
Beside him the boyar Peninsky
and the Chancellor Mikita Funikov.
Both are watching Euphrosyne and Kurbsky.
Is the old woman bringing him round? . . .
Eigh, that'd be good! After Kurbsky all would follow.
While as it is—their purpose wavers.

Euphrosyne is bending over Kurbsky:
Kiss the cross to Vladimir!
Both have turned round.

From behind a pillar of the staircase Malyuta is watching them.

Kurbsky has grabbed Euphrosyne by the arm.
Did he hear?
And Euphrosyne has replied soothingly:
He won't be able to report . . .

From the inner apartments emerge Pimen and the monks,
bearing the Holy Sacraments.

Malyuta calls the boyars to the Tsar:
The Tsar commands . . .

The boyars are on the move toward the inner apartments.
After them, her head raised royally, Euphrosyne,
the old Peninsky, Funikov, Vladimir Staritsky.

Her head flung back, Euphrosyne moves forward with royal stride.
Before her, as before a Tsarina,
the boyars obsequiously make way.
They allow her to precede.
Only one has not moved out of her path; the plain,
the dark-clad, semi soldier—Basmanov.
Transfixed with sorrow, his eye never wavers from the Tsar's door.
Euphrosyne pays no heed to him.

The forceful old woman bears down upon him.
She contracts her brows in anger.
With her staff she has pushed away Basmanov:
in silence and respect Basmanov moves to one side.

From the gorgeous, golden, boyar flood he draws aside.

Suddenly next to Kurbsky
appears the dark figure of the Livonian Ambassador:
And should aught betide—King Sigismund would always be glad.
He is eager for talented military commanders . . .
The King has great plans . . .

Kurbsky has moved past him to the Tsar's bedchamber.

99

IVAN'S BEDCHAMBER

Ivan lies in a fever.
At his bedside, Anastasia.
To one side, a cradle containing the infant Dmitry.
In a corner, the grim Malyuta.
Beneath an icon case the monk's habit lies ready . . .
Seven candles burn, embedded in a seven-branched candlestick.
At the head of the bed is a tall monk from Solovyets.

The boyars enter.

Ivan, barely moving his lips, says with an effort:
. . . The end has come . . .
I am taking leave of the world . . .
Kiss the cross to my heir . . .
the lawful heir . . .
Dmitry . . .
Ivan weakens.

Anastasia weeps.

Defiantly gaze back at Ivan, Euphrosyne Staritsky
and her son Vladimir.

Ivan reads refusal in their eyes.
He raises himself on the bed.
Anastasia supports him.

Ivan demands:
Kiss the cross to my son Dmitry . . .

The boyars are silent.

Ivan implores:
Kiss the cross to my son . . .

The boyars are silent.

Ivan with tears in his eyes urges them:
Not for my sake.
Not for my son:
but for the Russian land I beg you.
Only a power united—
bound by ties of blood—
can protect Moscow.
From foes.
From carnage.
Else the Tartars again will encroach upon us.
The Polish-Livonian power advance against us! . . .

The boyars are silent.
Ivan rises from the bed.

Throws himself on his knees.

From his knees, his face streaming with tears,
he appeals to the boyars.

He appeals to each individually:
Ivan Shuisky . . .
Peter Shchenyatov . . .
Semyon Rostovsky . . .

The boyars turn away.

Yet more feverishly,
yet more desperately,
Ivan appeals to the boyars:
Ivan Turuntay-Pronsky,
set an example!

Turuntay answers not a word.

Nemoy-Obolensky!
Why are you silent?

Obolensky turns away.

Kurletov!
Funikov!

A terrible attack of fury chokes Ivan.
He raises himself to his feet.

He shouts at the boyars:
For this, for all time
accursed be!

He loses consciousness.
He falls.

No one goes to his aid.

Alone Anastasia busies herself about him.
Malyuta stretches out his feet upon the bed.

Ivan in a dead faint.

And suddenly,
forgetting her shyness,
pale,
Anastasia draws herself to her full height.
She turns to the boyars:
Only in Dmitry—his son—lies salvation.
If there is no united power above you,
then though you be strong,
be you also brave,
though you be wise,
yet shall your rule be as chaos:
hating one the other,
foreign governance you'll serve.

Anastasia's cheeks are burning.
Her face is lit with conviction.
The pallor has fled from her features.

For her fledgling the dove offers battle.
For the great work of her husband she stands like an eagle.

From the doorway, not hearkening to a word,
Kurbsky adores Anastasia . . .

Like a lioness aroused, Euphrosyne has quit her place.
Like a lioness aroused, she bears down on the dove.
Mother against mother,
to defend her offspring she has risen:

Never shall the boyars, glorious, of ancient lineage,
lie beneath a Glinsky heel!

And the boyars look on in agreement:
We must kiss the cross to Vladimir Staritsky!

Mother advances against mother.
Mother before mother retreats.
A mother glares hatred into a mother's eyes . . .

Anastasia protects with her body the cradle containing Dmitry.

Dmitry is sleeping peacefully.

Ivan lies motionless.

Vladimir simpers.
Louder grows the boyar murmur:
We must kiss the cross to Prince Vladimir.

Euphrosyne snarls. She bears down on the Tsarina.
Anastasia defensively protects Dmitry with her body.

A shudder runs through Ivan . . .

But he lies motionless . . .
Only his fingers move, digging deep into the blanket.

Kurbsky shifts in the doorway.
His eyes have met Anastasia's.
Anastasia looks at him imploringly;
with her gaze she begs protection.

Between the Tsarina and Euphrosyne stands Kurbsky.
His gaze is fixed on Ivan.

With eyes bloodshot, Malyuta follows Kurbsky's every motion.

Now cries out the old boyar Peninsky—
of the retinue of the Staritskys—
voicing the general verdict:
The power must pass to a boyar Tsar!

So that authority shall be shared with the boyars!
And the boyar will prevail!

The clumsy lubber
Prince Vladimir Staritsky
simpers with satisfaction.

And Euphrosyne cries:
All must kiss the cross to Tsar Vladimir!

Ivan shudders.
But Ivan lies like one dead.

Kurbsky with steady gaze looks into his face.
He bends over him.

The face of Ivan, stonelike, deathlike.
Only drops of cold sweat upon his brow.

Kurbsky's doubts are assuaged.
He tears away his gaze.
He breaks into the boyar hubbub.
Looking at Anastasia, he bids all go from the chamber.
Noisily the boyars go out.
Kurbsky after them.

As though stung, Tsar Ivan raises himself on his elbow.
He gazes after the boyars.
The Tsar is in a fever, but the life in his look
is, at the least measure, trebled.
Malyuta has jumped forward.

Anastasia has gone to Ivan.
She has laid him down.
Malyuta, calm again, is watching Ivan.

FADE OUT

The door of the bedchamber suddenly opens.
Mightily enfeebled,
leaning on Anastasia and Malyuta,

appears Tsar Ivan:
The Holy Sacraments brought me succor . . .

The boyars are worried.
Ivan approaches Kurbsky,
Andrew stands in fear before the Tsar.

Ivan speaks:
You were as first before the Tsar. But yet higher shall you be exalted.
To you I assign the most notable duty of all.
With Kazan, with the East, it is finished,
and you, Kurbsky, shall lead the Russian forces . . .
to the West. To Livonia! To the sea!
He embraces Kurbsky.

And it is as though we can hear the voice of his old nurse:
> *Ocean-sea,*
> *Azure sea,*
> *Azure sea,*
> *Russian sea* . . .

Kurbsky over the shoulder of Ivan
meets the gaze of Anastasia.

Black is the gaze of her bright eyes:
she reads the soul of the Prince.

With a sharp turn of the head she averts her gaze.

Kurbsky has also turned away his head.
Eye to eye, his gaze has met that of Malyuta.
The face of Malyuta is laden with mistrust.
His eyes flash hatred.
Kurbsky lowers his glance.
And hastily bows before Ivan.

All shout to Kurbsky: *Glory!*

Ivan continues:
And to guard our southern borders from the Crimean Khan
I appoint . . .

All are holding their breath: to whom will he render this great honor?

Says Ivan:
. . . *Alexey Basmanov* . . .
Who's that? To whom?—is borne along the rows
of puzzled boyar corpulence.

In the doorway has modestly appeared Basmanov.
He is clad plainly: darkly, like a soldier . . .
All look at him with wonder.
Not looking aside at anyone, Basmanov has come up to Ivan.
He has kneeled down.

The Tsar has placed his hand on Basmanov's shoulder. He rests his
weight upon it.
With heavy gaze Tsar Ivan encompasses those present.

SLOW FADE-OUT

QUICK FADE-IN
THE STARITSKYS' MANSION

The Tsar trusts no one!
The boyars close to the throne he thrusts aside!
Quite unknown people he draws close to him!
To them he shows trust!—

the boyars bewail to Euphrosyne.
Amidst them Euphrosyne
stands like a stone statue.
I know—she says.

Land from ancient patrimonies to new upstarts
he transfers.
He persecutes the boyars!
Shchenyatov has been imprisoned!
Kurletov arrested!

I know—says Euphrosyne.

I shall flee!—shrilly cries Turuntay-Pronsky.
I can't stand it. I'm afraid. I shall escape to Lithuania.

For shame, Ivan Turuntay—says Euphrosyne—
The Metropolitan has gone to the Tsar:
he is interceding . . .

The doors are flung open.
The Metropolitan himself is in the doorway.
Quickly he comes into the chamber.
He drops onto a low bench.

Euphrosyne has run to him.
The others cluster round.

Says Pimen, breathing heavily,
whether from running,
or whether from wrath:
He spares no one . . .
I, the intercessor,
he has deprived of office . . .
He is transferring me from Moscow to Novgorod . . .

I shall flee! . . . —cries Turuntay-Pronsky—
By the Holy Cross—I shall flee!

He dashes from the chamber.
Past the flabbergasted boyars.

Those who are cowards, let them run—
the old Staritsky woman screeches after him.
He who stays shall fight.

Two boyars have fled hurriedly in Turuntay's wake . . .
The remainder have closed in around Pimen.

Says Pimen hotly:
While Ivan's close friend—

Kurbsky—
is far off . . . the opportunity must be seized to deal with the Tsar.

An aside has dropped from Euphrosyne:
The value of Kurbsky's friendship we shall yet learn . . .

Pimen instructs:
As a first task,
Ivan must be deprived of Anastasia . . .

All have dropped their eyes.
They stare in front of them.

The task is mine—I'll take it on myself . . .
says Euphrosyne.

She places herself on her knees before the icon.
She crosses herself with a wide cross . . .

                                        FADE OUT

IVAN'S APARTMENTS

A din.
Cursing.
Chinaware being broken.
Articles being smashed.

Ivan is seized with an access of wrath.
This is why they warily scamper away
into corners, tremble on staircases—
table servitors, bedchamber attendants, body servants of the Tsar.

Raging, foam on his lips, Ivan shouts:
The maritime cities, the Baltic cities, I must have them!

He runs over to a series of silver models of Riga, Narva, Reval.
Fixed on the models, the Swedish and Livonian arms
glitter brazenly.

Reval, Riga, Narva—I need them!
He is inflamed by the sight of the coats of arms.

Once more the Livonians,
Once more the Hansa traders,
have detained all wares from England.
Once more without lead, without sulphur, without tin, without trained
craftsmen

my cannon have been left helpless.

Ivan has grasped the silver Reval:
Reval! Thou S H A L T *be mine!*

The silver Reval has crashed to the ground.
It has shattered in fragments.
He has stamped upon the pieces.

Once again by a good Russian name—
Kolyvan—
shalt thou be known!

In her chamber hard by, Anastasia is indisposed:
burning fire wracks her; she lies in fever.

Euphrosyne Staritsky sits over her like a sable-hued bird.
She never moves her gaze from the sufferer.

Through cry and din the anger of Ivan reaches Anastasia.
Anastasia wants to rise,
to go to Ivan:
Let me to the Tsar. . . . He needs me . . .

Euphrosyne does not let her.
She makes her lie back.
Herself she listens.
The noise is dying down.

Ivan in his apartments.
He stands all moist with wrath.
He breathes heavily.

He throws himself down in a wide armchair.
He collects his breath.

He changes his voice.
He controls his anger.
To a shrewd-faced boyar, standing to one side,
he speaks thickly:
*You see, Nepeya, how much this military alliance
is necessary to me . . .*

He pushes over toward the boyar a luxurious set of chessmen:
Bear these as a gift
to our sweet sister Elizabeth
and, using them as pattern, you shall explain all to her . . .

Osip Nepeya enfolds the men in a silk handkerchief.

And you shall remind her that the Tsar Ivan at Moscow is the sole
merchant.
To whom he wishes—he gives leave.
Whom he wishes not—he allows not in his State.
Whom he fancies—to him he will open the road to the East . . .

He goes up to the boyar, dismisses him and shouts after him:
Further, take care that you do not drink too much, Nepeya:
What the sober man keeps in his head, the drunkard lets out on his
tongue . . .

Bowing deeply, Nepeya exits.

Behind the window—rain.
It is cold.
The Tsar shivers.
He wraps his fur cloak round himself.

In the chamber hard by, brooding over Anastasia, like a sable-hued bird,
sits Euphrosyne Staritsky.
Through the doorway she follows every movement of the Tsar.
She has recoiled with a start.
She has concealed herself on a stairway.

Ivan comes into the chamber.
Above Anastasia—eternal icon lamps in an arc.
Around—icon hangings embroidered by the Tsarina's own hands.
Ivan bends his head toward Anastasia . . .

Is Tsar Ivan worried?—says Anastasia.

She smooths Ivan's hair.
And, sick though she is, comforts the Tsar.

Says Ivan:
It is impossible to trust anyone.
Kurbsky is far: he fights in Livonia.
Kolychev is yet farther: he is praying in Solovyets.
You are all I have . . .

He bends lower.
He wishes to forget his troubles for a moment.

The Tsar is not allowed to forget,
The Tsar is not allowed to rest . . .
They run in with dispatches:
From Basmanov at Ryazan!

Ivan jumps up.
His eyes greedily devour the dispatch.
He takes in its contents:
THEY *again!*
He passionately complains to Anastasia:
Again the boyars set themselves to thwart our cause.
They are giving Basmanov and the people of Ryazan nothing for defense.
They are ready to surrender the city to the Crimean Khan!

Says Anastasia:
BE FIRM! . . .

Bitterly, Euphrosyne in the darkness hears the Tsarina's words.
Under the black kerchief on her bosom she fumbles.
She is groping for something . . .

Ivan rises. He says hotly:
I'll squeeze the boyars in this fist.
All land shall be allotted for service to the State!

The eyes of Euphrosyne have blazed with wrath.
With decision.
She slips out surreptitiously through a doorway . . .

Malyuta comes running in.
He speaks to the Tsar in a whisper:
Woeful news! The Russian army at Nevel is beaten.

He adds meaningly:
Kurbsky's been beaten . . .

Ivan lets fly.
Anastasia gives a cry.

Euphrosyne has stepped back into the apartment.

Anastasia feels suddenly ill.
She has been taken worse.

She twists on the bed.
She hangs over the bedside.
Near the floor she whispers:
. . . *It cannot be* . . .
It can't be . . .

Like a sable-hued shadow Euphrosyne stands in a corner.
In her hands she is holding a cup hidden by her kerchief . . .

Ivan rushes to Anastasia,
to give her a drink,
to bring her relief.
He turns to the beaker beside her.
The beaker is empty.
He stumbles, he twists—he seeks everywhere for water.

Carefully Euphrosyne stands her cup in the path of Ivan.

She looks out of the corner of her eye at Malyuta:
Malyuta notices nothing; he is plunged in deep thought.

Ivan snatches up the cup.
He carries it to the Tsarina.

Euphrosyne conceals herself in a corner. She watches from the corner.

Anastasia drinks thirstily from the cup.
Her eyes are wide open in fear.
Ivan holds the cup solicitously . . .

Euphrosyne crosses herself in her corner
with a tiny cross.
She whispers:
There is yet a God in Russia . . .

Hastily she hides an empty phial in her bosom.
In the darkness she noiselessly slips away . . .

FADE OUT

THE PALACE OF SIGISMUND

A luxurious tapestried hall.
A ceremonial atmosphere.
Fanfares.

The scene begins almost like the scene of Ivan's coronation.
Something is happening OFF SCREEN.
And various groups look OFF SCREEN.

Three German knights in armor.
A tall monk in a white robe.

A group of court ladies.
One of them—plump, in black velvet.
In widow's weeds.
Indistinguishable from a Gospel in a costly binding.
Her silhouette recalls that of Catherine de' Medici.
Such, most probably, was Anna Golshansky—

herself thrice a widow
and, in the future, the second wife of Kurbsky, widower.
Behind her—four pale ladies.
Two—in white.
Two—in black.
A pair of effeminate courtiers.

And above them, lit by reflections—
ponderous black figures of knights on horseback
woven in the tapestry.

In the foreground
a huge white and black ball.

Clustered around it—striped jesters.
The jesters keep glancing OFF SCREEN.
And tinkle their bells.

The jesters are mimicking what is happening in the background,
as yet invisible to the spectator.

Two jesters are balancing on the ball.
One of them—the chief, browless and moonfaced—
brandishes high his beribboned jester's wand.
A third bends the knee before the ball.
The first jester dangles in front of the kneeler his wand with the ribbon,
as though to invest the latter's neck with the decoration on its end.
He knocks the second jester off the ball by pushing him from behind.
The second jester falls.
A fourth jester takes a running leap over the ball.
The ball rolls.
The jesters fall in a heap one on top of the other. They freeze motionless.

The background has been revealed.
We see the throne of Sigismund II—Sigismund Augustus.

The King stands up.
He holds in his hand a ribbon with a glittering cross.

On his knees before the King—
Kurbsky with sword extended hilt foremost.
The King hangs the cross on Kurbsky.

He returns him his sword.

Close to Kurbsky—the Livonian Ambassador.
The old diplomat says unctuously:
Sometimes a defeat is a brilliant victory.
Kurbsky kisses the King's hand.

And triumphantly asserts:
In Moscow all are ready to come over to the side of Lithuania.
The defeat of the Russian troops at Nevel
will be the signal for revolt.
The Tsar's army is far to the south.

119

Tsar Ivan is like a bear
on all sides in his own den
surrounded.
It is possible to take him with one's bare hands . . .

The knights lean forward.
The monk listens intently.

Kurbsky continues:
The throne will be free,
For a new Tsar—
a friend of Poland. . .
The Prince looks at Sigismund expectantly.

Sigismund looks back at him enigmatically,
rises and proclaims:
On a Holy
Crusade
of all Christian States
we shall go up against Moscow!

A general *Vivat!*

The trumpets blare.

FADE OUT

A DARK CATHEDRAL INTERIOR.
NIGHT

A coffin with the body of Anastasia.
A voice in the darkness is reading in whispers a psalm—
a Psalm of David, the 69th:
> *Save me, O God;*
> *for the waters are come in unto my soul* . . .
The coffin is not made from boards but hollowed out,
carved, from the whole trunk of an oak.
It is draped with a black pall.

The psalm is heard:

I sink in deep mire
where there is no standing:
I am come into deep waters,
where the floods overflow me . . .
Ivan in deep sorrow beside the coffin.
I am weary of my crying:
my throat is dried:
mine eyes fail . . .
The psalm is intoned in a whisper by a monk standing behind the
lectern.

The words of the psalm intermingle with words spoken by Malyuta.
Malyuta is reading a dispatch.

Ivan's eyes are fixed on Anastasia.
He has no ears for either the dispatch or the prayer.

But the dispatch is disturbing:
Prince Ivan Shuisky
has taken refuge on Lithuanian soil . . .

Prince Ivan Sheremetyev
has been captured in flight . . .

Boyar Ivan Tugoy Luk of Suzdal
has escaped to Livonian territory . . .

In a whisper, the monk:
They that hate me without a cause
are more than the hairs of mine head
Calm is the countenance of the dead
Ivan gazes at her with yearning.
In his misery he flings himself on the ground.

In a whisper, Ivan:
Am I right in what I am doing?
Am I right?
Is this not the chastisement of God?

The monk continues:
I am become a stranger unto my brethren,
and an alien unto my mother's children . . .
Malyuta continues:

Prince Ivan Turuntay-Pronsky
has been captured in flight.
He has been turned back . . .
He has been brought back here . . .

Ivan rises from the ground.
He fixes his gaze on the dead countenance.
Am I right in this hard struggle of mine?

123

The dead countenance of Anastasia is silent.
And Tsar Ivan strikes his forehead on the edge of the coffin.

> *When I wept, and chastened my soul with fasting,*
> *that was to my reproach . . .*

The elder Basmanov runs into the cathedral.
With him is his son Fyodor.

> *I made sackcloth also my garment;*
> *and I became a proverb to them.*

The Basmanovs run up to Malyuta.
They have whispered in his ear.
Malyuta is startled.

> *They that sit in the gate speak against me;*
> *and I was the song of the drunkards.*

Malyuta has fallen on his knees before Ivan.
The treachery of Kurbsky is reported:
Kurbsky has gone over to Sigismund . . .

Ivan has raised his head.
His eyes are fixed far off in an uncomprehending stare.

He has understood.
Swiftly, in a whisper, he speaks:
Andrew, my friend . . . why?
Did aught not suffice thee?
Or didst thou covet my Royal Cap? . . .

The monk, in a whisper:
> *Deliver me out of the mire,*
> *and let me not sink:*
> *let me be delivered from them that hate me,*
> *and out of the deep waters . . .*

But Malyuta whispers to Ivan of worse yet:
Against you the boyars afresh
are inciting the people.
The Livonian defeat
has resulted in confusion and bewilderment . . .

The monk, in a whisper:
> *Reproach hath broken my heart;*
> *and I am full of heaviness . . .*
> *And I looked for some to take pity,*
> *but there was none;*
> *and for comforters,*
> *but I found none . . .*

Ivan has turned his head.

And he roars, like a wounded beast, to the whole Cathedral:
Thou liest!

The monk who was saying the psalm has been startled.
He has upset the lectern.

Through the whole Cathedral rings the proclamation:
The Moscow Tsar is not broken yet!

At the shout there run to Ivan those
who remain of the ones most near to him.
They are few—they are lost in the emptiness of the Cathedral . . .

Ye are few!—cries Ivan.
And he bids:
Summon to me my true friend, the last, the only one—

Kolychev.
In the far Solovyets Monastery
he prays for us!

Tsar! Trust not Boyar Kolychev—
Alexey Basmanov, the taciturn one, passionately urges the Tsar:
Surround yourself with new people.
All beholden to you.
Forge from them around you an iron ring
with sharp spikes presented to your enemies!

Ivan listens eagerly.

Basmanov goes on:
Forge it from such as shall forswear
their kith and kin,
their sires and mothers,
know none but the Tsar,
obey no will but the Tsar's!

He has taken hold of his son—Fyodor.
He has pushed him down onto his knees in front of the Tsar:
As first to be part of that iron ring.
for that great cause,
my own-born son, my only son,
his mother's only child,
I give to you!
Ivan listens eagerly to Basmanov the father.
Basmanov the son trembles to the roots of his hair.

Fyodor is sturdy: rough he is, and tough.
Wide-open eyes gaze at Ivan:
they are burning in an ecstasy of devotion.

Alexey goes on:
With them alone you will maintain power.
With them alone you will break the boyars.
Crush the traitors.
Accomplish your great task.

Ivan hears him greedily:
Thou speakest truthfully, Alyoshka!

We shall girdle Ourself with an iron ring.
We shall gather round Ourself an iron brotherhood.
Except for these men, my own, apart,* I shall trust none.
And I to them shall be their iron abbot . . .

Ivan's eyes flash with a clever thought,
his mind flying ahead of Basmanov:
Moscow I'll quit.
I'll go from it.
I'll go to the Alexandrov Liberty† . . .

The eyes of Malyuta have flashed back in reply:
Launch a march on Moscow . . .

Return as conqueror—
Alexey Basmanov cries.

But Ivan bends towards his comrades-in-arms:
No, we shall not return by a march . . .

They stand dumbfounded.

The Tsar continues:
We shall not return by a march . . .
We shall come back summoned by the people!

Basmanov and Malyuta are both perplexed . . .
Where is the Tsar's mind taking him?

Basmanov objects energetically:
You cannot await a summons from the people!

And Malyuta grumbles reproachfully:
You cannot listen to a mob.
Nor put your faith in ragged riffraff!

---

* These were the *Oprichniki*, men of the *Oprichnina*, which was one of two estates of the realm into which Ivan at this time divided Muscovy. He retained the *Oprichnina*—the "estate apart"—for his absolute personal use and service.
† A "Liberty" in medieval times was a suburb outside the city walls where the population was exempted from various rules and taxes.

The anger of the Tsar has been roused:
Thou forgettest thyself, ginger cur!
Thou presumest to teach the Tsar
how he should act?!

He speaks in wrath:
. . . in that summons—
I shall find power unlimited.
A new anointing, that I shall use
for the great cause—
RELENTLESSLY!

Ivan seeks support for his unprecedented idea.
He finds none from his comrades-in-arms.
Gloomily Malyuta fixed his gaze on the ground.
Gloomily at the ground stares Basmanov.

The Tsar's nearest are far from him—
they do not agree with the Tsar.

Ivan seeks approval for his unheard-of plan.
He finds none from those most near to him.
To his true companion—
his counselor—
to Anastasia he turns.

But Anastasia's dead countenance is silent:
her eyelids lowered . . .

Only one gaze gleams in the darkness of the Cathedral.
Unwaveringly it is fixed upon the Tsar:
the gaze of Fyodor Basmanov.

"Speak then!"

Fyodor replies firmly:
"You are right!"

Malyuta and Alexey Basmanov have given an indignant start,
but Ivan has flown to the platform like an arrow.

He hangs suspended above the coffin.
He gazes into the dead features.

The lines of the dead face seem to soften.
The face of Anastasia seems to shine with approval.

And not with grief now, but with decision,
Ivan gazes at that face.

Basmanov whispers to his Fedka:
Swiftly indeed have you grown into a Tsar's Man,
heeding none other . . .

Fixedly Fyodor is gazing at the Tsar:
he does not hear his father . . .
Swiftly have you changed father for father . . .

Music rises:
the theme of Ivan The Terrible—
"The Approaching Storm . . ."

Ivan straightens himself above the coffin.
His eyes burn with a new strength,
with resolution.
His hand passes above Anastasia.
And he swears a great oath.

In this summons from the people
I shall read the will of the Almighty
Into my hands I shall take the Lord's avenging sword.
The great task I shall accomplish:
a Sovereign almighty upon earth shall I become!

Broader in the orchestra grows the theme of The Terrible—
"The Approaching Storm."

The Cathedral has become alive with the blaze of torches.
The arches of the Cathedral are ringing with sound.
Through the Cathedral hurry torchbearers.
They are making ready for the Tsar's great cause.

High in the blaze of the light stands Ivan.
He speaks:
Two Romes fell,
but the third—
M o s c o w—
shall stand.
And a fourth Rome
shall never be!

The orchestra's trumpets blare the theme of The Terrible—
"The Approaching Storm" . . .

In the glare—Ivan.
Behind Ivan:
Malyuta, Basmanov.
Full of determination.
Fyodor.
Ivan kisses Anastasia on the forehead.

FADE OUT

FADE IN

THE OUTSKIRTS OF MOSCOW

The outskirts of Moscow are covered in snow.
Through the snow come sledge upon sledge in a train.
The runners creak.

But this train is no ordinary train—
it is an extraordinary one.
It bears not fish, nor salt, nor grain.
Under the matting covers gleam icon frames.
Under the matting are piled dishes.
Under the matting go coffers—
their beaten-metal sides glitter.

Mounted retainers escort the train on its flanks.

Retainers with halberds stand on the runners of the sledges;
the sledges are not ordinary ones—
they are the Tsar's.

In one of them the profile of the Tsar flashes by.
The profile of Tsar Ivan, muffled in a fur cloak.

The people run after the sledges.
They are perplexed.
They understand nothing of what has happened.

The Tsar's servants repeat only:
The Tsar is renouncing his kingdom . . .
He is leaving the boyar traitors—
Leaving the betrayers . . .

The sledges have passed beyond the outskirts.

The train of the Tsar has vanished in the distance.

The people are perplexed.
They whisper.

Abandoned Moscow is silent.

A whisper spreads through empty Moscow:
. . . The Tsar has abdicated . . .
The Tsar has gone . . .

THE ALEXANDROV LIBERTY

Beneath the gloomy vaults appears the face of Ivan.
A song resounds:
> *Before God I swear*
> *A faithful oath,*
> *A weighty oath,*
> *A fearful oath.*

Here beneath the vaulted ceilings of the Alexandrov Liberty
the Tsar's Men are gathered
to swear an oath.
In their hands they hold lighted candles.
They stand in a semicircle:
repeating after the elder Basmanov the words of the oath.
THE TSAR'S MEN:
> *Before God I swear*
> *A fearful oath . . .*

BASMANOV:
> *To serve the Sovereign of Russia like a dog.*

THE TSAR'S MEN:
> *Its towns and villages to sweep with a broom.*

BASMANOV:
> *Villainous scoundrels to tear with my teeth.*

THE TSAR'S MEN:
> *At the Tsar's command to lay down my bones.*

TOGETHER:
> FOR THE SAKE OF THE GREAT RUSSIAN REALM . . .

The Tsar's Men stand in a semicircle.
With lighted candles.
Habited all in black . . .

Against a table, brooms are leaning.
On the table, heads of dogs.
In front of it the elder Basmanov
holds a cup.

Fyodor is the first to pronounce the words of the oath:
> *Before God I swear*

133

A faithful oath:
To destroy the enemies of the State,
To renounce kith and kin,
Forget sire . . .
Steadily the Basmanovs look at each other:
father and son.
  . . . and own mother,
  True friend, blood brother,
  FOR THE SAKE OF THE GREAT RUSSIAN REALM.
Ivan towers like a black shadow.
He does not hear the oath.
He is lost in thought.
He examines his thin fingers.

Are you waiting for a messenger from Moscow?—
Malyuta whispers to the Tsar.

The Tsar moves suddenly towards Malyuta.
He seems to be listening to far-off Moscow.
From the distance he hears nothing.

Only the oath reverberates under the vaulted ceilings:
  Before God I swear
  A weighty oath:
  To execute throughout Russia the will of the Tsar,
  To destroy throughout Russia savage robbers,
  To shed throughout Russia the blood of the guilty,
  To burn out treason with fire,
  To cut out treachery with the sword,
  Not self nor others sparing—
  FOR THE SAKE OF THE GREAT RUSSIAN REALM.

The door has opened—
Boyar Nepeya
is at the feet of the Tsar:
Ships—
from England—
have sailed into the White Sea!

Ivan's eyes are shining with joy.
He has clenched his fists.
He has risen to his full height.

And from far, far off—
comes a sound like the singing of a church choir
in the distance.

As though reflecting the Tsar's delight,
the blades of the Tsar's Men are gleaming—
the Tsar's Men have drawn their daggers:

> *If I should break this fearful oath,*
> *Then may my brother Tsar's Men pierce me*
> *Mercilessly with their sharp daggers . . .*

BASMANOV THE SON:

> *Then may I be overtaken by the penalty of death.*

BASMANOV THE FATHER:

> *And by curses, and the tortures of Hell.*

BASMANOV THE SON:

> *And by shame, and the torments of the damned.*

THE TSAR'S MEN:

> *Then may green mother earth reject me.*

The echo rolls hollowly through the vaulted chambers.
With it, more clearly now, the far-off singing
of many voices
merges.
The Tsar hears the singing from afar.
Eagerly he listens to the singing.

Then the oath taken under the vaulted ceilings is finished.
It blends with the far chorus.

THE TSAR'S MEN:

> *May this my fearful oath before God*
> *Remain inviolable to the end of time,*
> *On earth as in Heaven—*
> FOR THE SAKE OF THE GREAT RUSSIAN REALM . . .

The Tsar's Men have fallen silent . . .

Basmanov the father declares
against the background of the distant chorus
coming nearer:

> *And may it stand for ages eternal*
> *Inviolable for ever and ever.*

Amen!—
concludes the Tsar.

The door has been flung open.
Malyuta has rushed in.

A beam of light enters from the door
and the roar of the singing pilgrimage
bursts in.

Ivan goes out through the beam of light.
In the midst of a vast snowy expanse,
flooded by the sun,
he stands on the roof.

Before him in an endless stream
stretches the pilgrimage from Moscow . . .
With crosses,
with icons,
with sacred banners,
it glitters against the snow.

The people see the Tsar.

Their singing ceases.
They fall on their knees.

Return to thy kingdom!—
a voice cries beseechingly.

Dear father of ours!—
voices join in.

Ivan draws himself erect.
His nostrils dilate.

With heads bowed, there stand
Pimen,
Euphrosyne,
Vladimir,
and five more boyars.

All their voices as one:

RETURN!—
the people cry.
The theme of the "Terrible" expands in the music.

Suddenly, slyly,
to those nearest him—
to the Tsar's Men—
the Tsar smiles:
*Saddle the horses
to gallop to Moscow!*

From a swift MIX
cries of *Holla! Holla!*

Over the snowy hills
pours raven-hued lava:

In a black cloud tear along
riders fantastic.

Clad in long black tunics,
on their saddles, brooms and dogs' heads,
The "TSAR'S MEN."

In the orchestra the theme of The Terrible swells to a roar.
Among the riders, on horseback also,
the Tsar himself.

Terrible is the Tsar's aspect.
The Tsar has grown haggard.
He has aged.
His eyes blaze.
Behind him whirl the Basmanovs,
Malyuta.

Holla! Holla!
In a black cloud against the snow
the riders furiously tear forward . . .

                                        FADE OUT

END OF PART ONE

IVAN THE TERRIBLE

PART TWO

THE OUTSKIRTS OF MOSCOW

The credits appear against the rising music of the song.
"Ocean-sea, Azure sea."

A title appears:

IN THE YEAR 1565 ON THE 3RD OF FEBRUARY
THE TSAR CAME BACK . . .

With the title still on the screen, there bursts out sharply
the cry *Holla! Holla!*
Piercing whistles.

AND QUICKLY FADES IN

A snow-covered waste . . .
The sound of whistling and hollaing.
Holla! Holla!

Across the snow-clad slopes
a black lava pours towards us:
in a raven mass, rushing out of the distance,
the riders fantastic.

Clad in long black tunics.
Brooms and dogs' heads on their saddles.
Amidst the riders, on horseback also—the Tsar himself.

He has grown haggard.
He has aged,
His eyes blaze.

Behind him career the Basmanovs. Malyuta.
At the outskirts of Moscow
the people fall to their knees.

Terrible is the Tsar:
he does not look upon the people.
In wrath he whirls past them.

In a raven cloud the riders pour by . . .

THE HALL OF AUDIENCE

And behold they stand one against the other,
like hosts drawn up for battle.

On the one side—the boyars in gold.
On the other—in a black bevy, the Tsar's Men.

Between them
Tsar Ivan walks.

The aspect of the Tsar has changed.
He has grown haggard, aged.
Changed also is the royal speech.
It has grown full of bile,
caustic.

So? You fell into the trap? Didn't expect me back?
You rejoiced when the Tsar went away?
You've given yourselves away, neck and crop, traitors . . .
To rule over the land yourselves was your desire?
He has halted opposite the embarrassed boyars.
Well, so be it, then!
Henceforward I yield the Russian lands to you for government.
"Lands' Men" * *I name you.*

A movement among the boyars.

Once more the Tsar has walked between the boyars and the Tsar's Men.
To the boyars bent, subdued, he says:
And of those lands bereaved,
as widower's portion—
small, the exception—
for myself I keep:
the towns on the periphery: Byelyov, Kozelsk, Vorotinsk—
the heart of the Vorotinsky, Odoyevsky and Byelyovsky princedoms.
Suzdal, Vyazma, Mozhaisk—on the roads to Lithuania;
Staraya Russa—on the road to the Baltic,
the Maritime Region as far as the White Sea . . .

Distinctly he has pronounced:
. . . Yaroslavl . . .
He continues:
With these towns the safety of the State
I shall preserve.
To guard the Russian borders . . .

He has stopped.
Keeping his voice low,
barely audibly, deliberately, he has spoken:
. . . Also, to stamp out treason . . .
His glance passes along the ranks of the boyars.

* Men of the *Zemshchina*, the "Estate of the Land," where traditional ranks would
remain, subject to the autocracy Ivan was asserting. The speech is ironical: Ivan is
graciously giving the boyars land that was before, in practice, absolutely their own, to
administer now as his agents.

A shudder has passed through their ranks.

Once again the Tsar has walked past the boyars.
He stares at them.
He speaks:
And since in you, boyars,
I place no trust . . .
. . . as my own executants of the royal will,
like Adam by the Lord
raised from the dust . . .
He has ascended the throne:
. . . SINCE I TRUST NONE APART FROM THESE—
I NAME THESE "MEN APART"—THE TSAR'S MEN.

He has indicated the Tsar's Men.

In black ranks the Tsar's Men
stare at the boyars.
Malyuta,
Basmanov the elder,
Basmanov the son,
a company of stalwarts,
habited in black.

At the boyars stare the Tsar's Men . . .

Horror seizes the boyars.

From the midst of the boyars, suddenly,
Abbot Philip emerges.

Ivan is delighted.
But Philip is stern.

He denounces the works of the Tsar:
Not from God are thy undertakings—
but from the devil!

He threatens:
And whosoever in his realm
its age-old customs overthrows—
For him it shall not long remain his realm!

Quiet, quiet, Prelate!—
cries Ivan anxiously,
fearing the outburst of his own anger.
And he hastily draws Philip to one side.

The Tsar's Men have moved against the boyars.
Fedka foremost.
The "Lands' Men" are hustled toward the exits by the Tsar's Men.

Alone by the royal throne,
face to face,

stand the onetime friends—
Ivan and Philip,
face to face.

Fedka and the Tsar's Men
press the "Lands' Men" into the palace corridors.
They handle roughly these "landed" gentry.

And in the audience hall the two yet stand.
One against the other—
as antagonists,
face to face:
the Tsar and the priest.

The Angel of Wrath
from the Apocalypse
is above them:
he is trampling the universe underfoot.

The Tsar wishes to embrace Philip.
Philip does not permit it.

He wishes to touch Philip,
but Philip is stern.

And Ivan cries to Philip
from his royal seat, with anguish:
Why are you stern with me, Fyodor Kolychev?
Why so cruel?
My friend!
To pity me were needed . . .

Philip does not look at him.
His stern gaze remains fixed on the ground.
He says:
I am the humble monk Philip.
I do the will of God,
and in thy affairs am not an adjutant . . .

Ivan is crushed down in the royal throne,
as once before, when but a child,
in that same place he sat in fear.

I had a dearest friend—Anastasia.
She left me.
I had a dear friend . . .
He hesitates. He does not utter the name.
He says thickly:
. . . he betrayed me . . .
Not me—but the great Cause . . .

A spasm runs like lightning across the face of Ivan.
His eyes twitch.
The neck retreats into the shoulders, exhausted.
In the folds of Philip's mantle
Ivan masks his face, in fear.

Not treason do I fear. Nor the knife.
Nor poison, nor betrayal . . .
For my own sake I am not fearful:
But fearful for the Cause, great,
young, just begun . . .

And the pale features
of the Tsar's yellowed face
suddenly show alarm—
childish,
juvenile. . . .

Looking past the Tsar, Philip replies
solemnly:
No destiny can be more great
than in accord with ancient sovereignty to rule.
According to the pattern of father, grandfather, great-grandfather
to govern.
To the boyars to hearken.
With the boyars to share power . . .

Swiftly Ivan's eyes have narrowed.
His lips have compressed—and separated:
You lie, black one! You babble nonsense!—
the words burst in fury from the Tsar.
Like lightning in the gathering twilight
his eyes flash.

But the priest is no coward, nor has he the docility
that might quiet him as the dove:
So, thou desirest not to hearken to a pastor?
Then sit alone . . .
And he intones, like a bell tolling anathema:
. . . *reviled, condemned,*
accursed! . . .
He has torn away his mantle. He breathes out icily:
. . . A L O N E !
And plunges toward the door.

Ivan catches at the mantle from his royal seat.
Clings to it desperately from the half-dark corner.
He does not release the pastor.
He makes toward Philip.
Stumbles on the mantle.
Trips.
Finds himself unexpectedly at Philip's feet.

He pulls the pastor toward him.
Begs him piteously:
I plead with you not as Tsar but as a friend
weighed down by the heavy burden of power . . .

Philip is silent.
He stands motionless.
But his eyes soften.

Seeing this, the Tsar, toward Philip,
presses nearer.
Clutching the mantle more tightly:
Do not cast me into loneliness.
Be with me:
help me strengthen the Russian State . . .

By now all around is almost dark.

And take for yourself here in Moscow
the Moscow bishopric . . .

Philip ponders deeply.

Anxiously the Tsar watches the abbot.

The brows on Philip's forehead contract.
Behind the brows his thoughts gather:
how to defend the boyars
being Bishop in Moscow . . .

He answers slowly:
Wilt thou grant me the right to intercede before thee?
To plead before thee for the condemned?
In turn he looks keenly at Ivan.

No one is condemned unjustly!—
Ivan is on the point of flaring up.
He damps down the fire.

With heavy heart, to Philip's request
Ivan accedes.

Painfully he bridles his stern temper.
For he feels: without this consent, Philip will depart
and he himself will once more be alone . . .

And he humbles his heart—digs his nails into his flesh.
Submits.
Bridling his strength,
and against his will, he bows his head:
agrees . . .

Philip's eyes have lit up.
He stretches out his hand to Ivan.
Like friends—as in days past—
Tsar and prelate embrace.

Only not quite:
the Tsar smiles a half smile—
a purchased friendship does not rejoice him.
Not for such friendship does he yearn.
Not at such a price does he seek friendship . . .
Though he tries, yet he does not rejoice.

But the stern face of Philip
smiles from ear to ear.
Philip kisses the brow of the Tsar;
with the Tsar he is reconciled.
Peace concluded, an alliance.
He fails to notice Ivan's look.

Ivan's look therefore
grows darker than ever . . .

The pastor fusses about, glad in his victory.
He beckons to the acolyte—Eustace—beside him.
He presents him to the Tsar:
Take this pledge of new friendship:
this monk—Eustace—
I give thee as confessor.

Young is Eustace. Small of stature.
Blue-eyed. Radiant. Pure.

The Tsar hides the bitterness of his disappointment.

He takes leave of Philip.
Respectfully, to Philip's hand,
he presses his lips.

Proudly the priest stares above the head of the Tsar.
And, embracing the Tsar, goes off.

Eustace escorts Philip.

The Tsar has dropped his head.
He stands pondering . . .

Why such power over you
do you give to a priest?—
as though speaking the Tsar's thoughts aloud—
a hoarse voice pronounces from behind a pillar.

The Tsar has sharply turned round.

From under an arch Malyuta looks toward the Tsar:
Why do you accept such humiliation from an ecclesiastical churl?

*That's not your business, cur!—*the Tsar has rapped out.

Malyuta is unrecognizable.
He has not been silenced. He is not appeased.
Angrily he growls at the Tsar.
Cur? I know—a cur. A cur indeed am I.
But a devoted cur. Not a betraying cur.
In error you prefer a priest to a cur . . .

He comes closer:
I know—you seek friendship . . .
Without friends you sorrow . . .

Ivan is thunderstruck by this boldness.

But Malyuta continues. Impetuously:
. . . And you fail to perceive
that Philip has but one aim:
to cover your foes from your wrath with his cassock.
He mocks:

153

A fine friend!
I dare say, no better than Kurbsky!

Mastering himself, Ivan has groaned:
Don't dare name that name!

Ivan has flung himself into his throne.

Malyuta crawls up.
And whispers in the very ear of the Tsar,
narrowing one eye understandingly:
You have given your word to the priest—a promise.
I understand: your word you'll not take back . . .

Ivan is listening.

MALYUTA:
I understand . . . you need to act in such wise
that the Royal Word remains unbroken . . .
yet the traitors are got rid of . . .

And then, he has put the question solicitously, as though to a little child:
. . . So, that is what's troubling you so? . . .

Ivan has bowed his head.

Malyuta whispers in the ear of the Tsar bent toward him:
. . . There is a way out: a serf, on his own . . .
Aye, not a serf . . . But just—a ginger cur . . .
does the job on his own . . .
He grows warmer:
A serf, on his own—Malyuta.
A cur, on his own—Malyuta
takes upon himself the whole of the dirt.
He flings back his head with pride.
I shall enter into the memory of the people as a byword of shame.
He says forcefully:
I shall lay down my soul for the Tsar.
My soul I shall damn,
but the sacredness of the Tsar's Word I shall preserve!
He bends his head before the Tsar . . .

Ivan has lifted Malyuta's face by the chin.

155

He has raised up his head.
He stares in the eye his faithful ginger dog.

Says Malyuta cunningly,
narrowing one eye, with deliberation:
What does a hunting dog do,
if a wild beast is cunning—
and flies for its lair like an arrow? . . .

Says Ivan meditatively:
He outstrips,
outleaps,
overtakes the wild beast . . .

Malyuta's thought catches on:
Outleap the priest . . . overtake him is your idea?
Set about it so that he'll have no time to intercede?

Malyuta does not like Ivan's pondering.
He sees disquiet in Ivan's eyes.
He makes haste and departs toward the exit,
so that Ivan shall not have time to reconsider,
so that Ivan shall not have time to change his mind.

Malyuta vanishes in the shadows.

Slowly Ivan rises from his chair.
He draws himself to his full height,
grasps his head between his hands.
Whispers to himself:
By what right do you judge, Tsar Ivan?
By what right do you wield the avenging sword? . . .

With sorrow, supplication, horror,
he stares into the vaulted arches above him.
He has raised his hands on high.

The huge black bear fur,
falling from his shoulders,
has coiled tamely at the foot of the armchair,
lain down, spread out.

Suddenly Ivan is all crumpled.
Shrunk into himself.
He starts to run clumsily through the Golden Hall.

He has run along the wide staircase,
vanished behind the arches.

From the doorway Malyuta peers after him.
He speaks to Fedka Basmanov:
Look after the Tsar:
don't let him be alone.

Ivan runs, breathing heavily, up the stairs.
He runs into the bedchamber of Anastasia, above.

ANASTASIA'S BEDCHAMBER

All is unaltered in the bedchamber.
The icon hangings, woven by the hand of the Tsarina . . .
By the bedstead the ever-burning icon lamps arranged in an arc . . .
The cup on the table,
just as it stood
at the death of the Tsarina . . .

Only the Tsarina is absent—
She is long in the tomb . . .

On his knees before the icon lamps the Tsar flings himself down.
Let this cup pass from me . . . he prays.

It'll not pass!—from behind the Tsar comes the voice of Fyodor:
Cups nowadays are filled with poison . . .

Ivan has leaped to his feet.
He has looked:

the cup is standing before the icon.
The cup which he himself gave Anastasia at her death.
The cup . . .

Ivan stares at the cup with crazed eyes:
She was poisoned?—he whispers.
She was poisoned—he shouts—*my beloved?*
He is about to fling himself to the floor.

Strong hands hold Ivan.
The hands of Fyodor Basmanov:
Be firm!

H E R W O R D S !—cries Ivan.

He has seized Fyodor.
Has gripped him tight.
Who was it that presented to the Tsarina this cup . . .
the last . . . *before her death?*

The Tsar's legs give way beneath him.
The Tsar sinks onto a couch.
He holds his hands out far in front of him:
From my hands she took it . . .
He gazes at his hands in horror.

Fyodor bends toward Ivan:
And who handed it to you?

Ivan leaps up:
E U P H R O S Y N E !—
he has screamed.

He has flung off his irresolution.
Come!—he cries.
He rushes off with Fedka.

Ivan, leading Fedka, dashes
down the stairs,
along the corridors.

He hurries to a secret window.
They open its secret iron shutter.

Framed in the secret window
under the stairs,
the eye of Ivan burns;
it glitters.

Under the window, Tsar's Men
haul boyars along with shouts.
They arc hustling them down steps.
Dragging them over snow . . .

Out on the snow—Malyuta,
stripped, bare, to the waist.

On their knees before him,
the boyars are flung down.

Three of them.
All kin of the Kolychevs.
Proud.

Tsar's Men, clad in black, are holding them.

The boyars are proud—their heads are unbowed.
Only the youngest—terrified—
shows the desire not to die.

Through the corridors, having seen off Philip,
Eustace is coming back.
He sees—in the courtyard—
Malyuta reading out the sentence:
. . . *For action treasonable to the State—off with their heads.*
The sword waves aloft.

With a cry Eustace races down the porch steps.
He runs out onto the snow. He runs up to Malyuta.
He grabs the sword in its swing.

*Stop, serf!—*he cries.
I am the spiritual adviser of the Tsar . . .
His bright eyes burn in frenzy.

The suddenness of this halts Malyuta.
His sword has stopped in its swing.
Eustace is pulling at his arm.

The condemned, surprised,
look on curiously:
for bystanders to meddle
in an execution is hardly meet.

The ginger jowl of Malyuta dissolves into a smile
He reveals an uneven row of teeth:
Spiritual adviser of the Tsar . . .

He rasps out suddenly:
And I'm his bodily adviser!

I care for the body and the business of the Tsar!
I'll not allow your priestly doubts
To enter his soul . . .

He thrusts out a heavy hand—a forty-pound fist:
And you, learn your place;
Don't poke your nose into State affairs.

Like a gnat,
like an importunate fly,
the new-fledged, ill-starred peacemaker
is swatted into the snow.

On the snow Eustace lies.
He watches, horrified, the strange spectacle.
So alien to monastery life.

With a whistle the sword takes off the head
of the first boyar . . .
of the second . . .
A pause; of the third—
the youngest.

With the first two, it swung in a circle parallel to the earth:
not bending their necks, the boyars had stood erect.

For the third—from above downwards:
in woe, his head inclined to earth,
the third, the youngest, had stood drooping.

Eustace's teeth chatter without stopping.
His pure eyes are suffused with radiant tears.

He crouches under the gate.
Shivering in the snow.

Malyuta wipes off his sword on the skirt of his coat.
He winks at Eustace:
See how Tsar Ivan
will thank me now.
He crosses the courtyard with wide strides.

The Tsar's Men, with curiosity,
glance at the bodies;
they discuss Malyuta's strokes.
They are astonished at their speed and accuracy.
They are astounded at their strength.

Malyuta ascends the palace corridors.
He sees
on the staircase, advancing to meet Malyuta, the Tsar himself.
The Tsar supports himself with one hand on the wall; he is coming to-
                                    ward the courtyard.
He is leaning on Fedka.

Proudly in the path of the Tsar stands Malyuta—he is awaiting approval:
the trace of a kiss burns on his brow like an invisible star.
Its more tangible twin—a real emerald—
Malyuta awaits for his cap . . .
To Fyodor he says:
See how the Tsar will now express his approval of me . . .

The eyes of Ivan are open wide.
He does not look at Malyuta.
Straight past Malyuta goes the Tsar.
The sight of the executed men engrosses him.
His long black fur cloak brushes the porch steps.
He gazes at the executed, abandoned to the blizzard.

The Tsar's Men have dropped their caps.
They bow, waist-low.
He does not look at them either . . .

Malyuta's whole being drinks in the Tsar with his eyes.
He draws himself up.
Like a dog on guard he stares at the Tsar:
see, any moment now, Ivan's eyes will gleam with delight.
See, any moment now, he will pour out thanks upon Malyuta.

But not this does the Tsar.
The eye of the Tsar does not burn with delight: it burns with grief.
The Tsar does not pour forth thanks:

he doffs his cap.
He crosses himself with a sweeping cross in memory of the dead.

Then suddenly:
Too few!—
he says.

Malyuta has vomited out an oath:
Too few for you? There shall be more, Tsar Ivan!

Dashing like hounds through the snowstorm,
stumbling across the corpses,
to the horses of black—their own color—
the Tsar's Men have rushed through the courtyard.

With a cry:
Holla, Holla!
plunging
in a black pack
from the Tsar's courtyard they have whirled away . . .

After them Fedka has flown like an arrow,
dodging on the run the dead bodies.
He has vanished in the snowstorm.

The Tsar stands alone.
He hears a distant whimper.

Eustace is sobbing in the gateway.

Past the bodies of the slain the Tsar goes to Eustace across the snow.
He lifts Eustace up.
He gazes with pity into the meek eyes of Eustace.
Covering Eustace with his fur cloak, he leads him back onto the porch
steps.
On the porch he comforts him;
part to himself, part to Eustace, he says:
Heavy is the task of a Tsar.
Harder than running a monastery.
Building a State is not like reading the Akathistos . . .

Eustace sobs, he whimpers.

163

By the Tsar's cloak,
as in the folds of a confessor's stole,
he is protected;
on the Tsar's breast he is warmed.
Through his tears he whispers:
At least give the bodies to their relatives for the last rites . . .

The snowstorm whistles through the courtyard. It howls.
In the depths of the courtyard the bodies of the executed are being re-
moved.
The traces of the execution are being swept away by the storm.

The storm rages through the courtyard.

It rages through Moscow city.
As though it were the Tsar of Muscovy
sweeping away treason with a storm . . .
The storm rages wrathfully.
The horses of the Tsar's Men are galloping.
With shouting through the blizzard,
the Tsar's Men are tearing forth
to wreak harsh justice.
The horses are galloping.

The storm is raging.
In a howl, the words of the storm
merge with the oaths of the Tsar's Men.

With a howl, the storm rollicks along the outlying streets.
Boyars, dragged like bundles, it escorts with laughter . . .

A boyar's wife makes haste to her home from a party.
Arrived panting, she sees—
the courtyard crowded with Tsar's Men.
And the boyar hanging from the gates of his own house.
Her senses fled, the boyar's wife has sunk down in the snow.

But the Tsar's Men drag through the courtyard the boyar's treasure
for the Tsar's treasury . . .
The elder Basmanov himself is supervising them.

And the younger Basmanov—Fedka—
through the smashed-up apartments

is chasing a maiden;
he has squeezed her into a corner.
Between them a table.
Fedka—over the table.
The girl is pinned in the corner.

The Basmanov hurls himself upon her . . .
He cries out unexpectedly:
You fool, I'm not after that . . .
I'm after your earrings!

This the lass did not in the least expect;
out of shame she flops down in a dead faint.

Fedka takes off her earrings.

Aides carry off the girl.

Fedka is admiring the earrings.
He himself is smartly dressed, combed.

Suddenly a heavy hand has seized Fyodor by the collar.
In front of Fedka stands—father Basmanov.

Drop them, Fyodor! Not for plundering were the Tsar's Men created.
But for the Tsar's justice and the Tsar's treasury.

He has taken the earrings from his son.
He has placed them in his own deep, capacious pocket . . .
Crushed, Fyodor has heaved a sigh.

In the background the boyar's goods are being carried off.
With shouts the Tsar's Men gallop on.

THE METROPOLITAN'S CELL

It is not light in the cell:
the night is dark.

The cell is packed with smoke:
candles innumerable are burning.

The cell is packed with noise:
a moaning and a groaning.
May they rest with the saints . . . is heard in the distance.

In the middle of the cell—Philip.

The boyars have surrounded Philip in a circle.
Hands are stretched out to Philip between the candles.
They beg protection.

Philip sits like a stone image.

Over him, ancient and angry,
Pimen of Novgorod
calls for vengeance:
With the priestly power, granted of God,
humble the Tsar.
Excommunicate the Tsar!

Philip sits motionless among the candles;
he stares in front of him at three coffins.

In front of him—the three open coffins.
Within them, the three bodies of the executed,
slain by Malyuta.
Philip sits above them like a stone image.
He does not listen to Pimen.
Despite fierce insult,
Philip is reluctant to go as far as a break with the Tsar:
I'll go back to the monastery . . .

Pimen objects:
Do not . . .
If thou curb'st not the Tsar,
before God thou'lt answer!

Philip sits like a stone image.
He says nothing.

The door is flung open:
the candles are blown by the draft from the door;
the flames of the candles leap,
as, from the doorway, onto her knees
Euphrosyne has fallen.
Together with Euphrosyne are her whole family.

On her knees, Euphrosyne, tearless, screams out to Philip:
Justice and protection
not for myself—but for the boyar cause I ask.
Nor ask, prelate—
demand!

Philip hears the fiery words,
the angry speeches, broken groans.
And inside Philip himself there grows,
beneath the cover of his meek shepherd's garb,
a wrath great, boyar, mutinous, warlike . . .

Not defense against the Tsar:
but a curb upon the Tsar I ask,
nor ask—demand!

167

May they rest with the saints—is heard in the distance.

Filled with gentleness, bowing to Euphrosyne,
Philip raises the old woman.

Risen from the floor, he straightens up.
Before the eyes of all he is transformed:
he stands erect, clipped,
his shoulders knightly,
like a boyar;
he sets his head
high,
Kolychev-style.

With Kolychev fire the eyes of the Metropolitan gleam.
With Kolychev ring the voice of Philip thunders:
God sees—
that not for myself,
not for my tormented kin—
but for the boyar cause I raise the sword:
there shall be justice on the Tsar!
Against the Church the Tsar cannot withstand.
Though I wear the cassock—I am yet a Kolychev!
Though I be a Kolychev—yet am I a Prince of the Church!!
Come tomorrow all
to the Furnace Play
in the Cathedral:
I'll bend the Tsar,
I'll humble him.
I'll crush him with the Church!

FADE OUT

FADE IN

THE CATHEDRAL. JOYFUL CARILLON.
THE FIERY FURNACE PLAY

Many people.
In the center of the Cathedral
where Ivan long ago delivered his speech,

the ambo—adapted for "The Fiery Chaldean Furnace."

A little boy asks his mother in a ringing voice:
And what is a "Fiery Furnace Play"?

Beside him stands Euphrosyne Staritsky.
She explains meaningfully:

The "Fiery Furnace Play" tells how the Angel of the Lord
delivered from the Chaldean fiery furnace
three youths—
Shadrach, Meshach and Abednego—
who had been cast into that fiery furnace
by the terrible Tsar of the heathens . . .

Nearby Prince Vladimir Staritsky has given a sigh:
Nowadays, alas, such angels are no more . . .

A general movement.
In front of the furnace there emerges, with other ecclesiastics,
Metropolitan Philip.
In the name of the Father, the Son and the Holy Ghost . . .
he has blessed the start of the play.

The boy has been lifted up onto a shoulder.

And now already one can see being led to the furnace three youths:
Shadrach, Meshach and Abednego.
The youths are bound with kerchiefs and towels.
Driving them with clownish grimaces
are two Chaldeans.

The youths have come to a stop on the ambo.
With angelic crystal voices
they sing in lamentation:
>   *We being innocent are now cast*
>   *By the Tsar of the heathens, for disobedience,*
>   *Into the burning*
>   *Fiery furnace*
>   *Heated by the Chaldeans.*
A group of boyars sigh sonorously.
Euphrosyne nudges them.

The youths move into the furnace.
In front of the furnace are the two Chaldeans.

1ST CHALDEAN:
Chaldean, O Chaldean!
2ND CHALDEAN:
What ails?
1ST CHALDEAN:
Is this the Tsar's doing?
2ND CHALDEAN:
Aye, the Tsar's.
1ST CHALDEAN:
They would not serve the Tsar?
2ND CHALDEAN:
Aye, would not.
1ST CHALDEAN:
So we cast them into the furnace.
2ND CHALDEAN:
And begin to consume them with fire.

The youths are now seen inside the furnace.
They have lit candles.
Beneath the furnace Chaldeans are lighting
fireworks
(they burn lycopodium).

Sing again the youths
Shadrach, Meshach and Abednego,
lit by the light of the candles.
Ring out their crystal voices:
> *Now are we betrayed*
> *Into the hands of a lawless ruler,*
> *By apostates most hateful,*
> *To a Tsar unrighteous*
> *And the most evil on all the earth.*
The voices reach from afar to the altar.
At the altar:
Philip in the Metropolitan's seat—
a throne of stone.

On his right—Pimen, Bishop of Novgorod.
On his left—the Bishop of Rostov.
A little way off:
the Bishops—of Ryazan and Suzdal.

The angelic singing of the youths is heard from the furnace:
>   *Today we have not*
>   *Either Tsar or prince*
>   *Righteous,*
>   *Pleasing to God,*
>   *Us youths to defend,*
>   *God's judgment to fulfil,*
>   *The haughty Tsar to humble* . . .
Whispers of approval amidst the boyars.
They look at Vladimir and Euphrosyne.

The angelic singing of the youths reaches the altar.
But the speech at the altar is far from angelic.
The Bishop of Rostov says excitedly to Philip:
Prince Turuntay-Pronsky
was making a sudden dash for Livonian soil.
He's been caught.
He's donned a martyr's crown . . .

He crosses himself.

And the lands of the Prince have been given over to Tsar's men . . .
All cross themselves in silence.
Philip's brows contract wrathfully:
Thou stridest wide, Tsar Ivan!

The singing of the youths is heard in the distance:
>   *Brought low are we, Lord,*
>   *Lower than all peoples,*
>   *And shamed now*
>   *Over all the earth* . . .
But Pimen of Novgorod has worse to communicate:
Yet more bitter than that—
the Tsar has for his treasury
church lands begun to confiscate.

Philip jumps up in a rage:

Thou stridest wide, on whom dost thou now trample:
against the Church thou'lt not prevail!

Though I wear the cassock—I am yet a Kolychev!
Though I be a Kolychev—yet am I a Prince of the Church!

I'll bend the Tsar. I'll humble him.
I'll crush him with the Church!

He draws himself up to his full height.
Stands wrathful by the Metropolitan's throne.

With their crystal voices the youths in the distance repeat:
> *Brought low are we, Lord,*
> *Lower than all peoples,*
> *And shamed now*
> *Over all the earth . . .*
But Peter, Pimen's novice, runs up.
He reports:
The Tsar is coming to the Cathedral . . .

Philip has moved angrily away from the altar.
The bishops with him.

The Tsar enters the Cathedral.
Tsar's Men with him.
Among them
Malyuta.
The Basmanovs—
father and son.

All have monkish cassocks thrown over them.
The Tsar wears a cowl.

To meet the Tsar
Philip comes forward.
He halts in front of the furnace.

Ivan accompanied by Tsar's Men
advances through the Cathedral.

The youths sing

with their crystal voices.
Without emotion,
without expression,
without comprehension of the sense of the words:
like a transparent angel choir.

And coming to meet the Tsar
these words soar forth:
> *Why, O Chaldeans shameless,*
> *A lawless Tsar*
> *Do you serve?*
> *Why, O Chaldeans diabolical,*
> *In a Tsar of Satan—*
> *An outrager, tormentor—*
> *Do you rejoice? . . .*

The Tsar has stopped.
He listens bewildered to the words.
Beside the Tsar is Fyodor Basmanov.
He seethes with anger.

Sing the youths:
> *Why with fires do you torture,*
> *With flames do you scorch . . .*

The Tsar's Men have stopped.

Ivan behaves as though he does not hear the words.
He approaches Philip for his benediction.

Philip turns away . . .

Thrice Ivan bows his head.
Thrice Philip turns away.

Wondering, the people watch.
They have caught their breath.

With crystal voices
the youths sing amidst the dead silence:
> *Now a miracle shalt thou see.*
> *There shall be cast down*
> *The Lord of Earth*
> *By the Lord of Heaven.*

173

Fyodor springs to Philip.
Says, remonstrating:
The Tsar of all Rus
asks benediction!

Sharply replies Philip:
I do not recognize the Tsar of the Orthodox
in un-Tsarlike raiment.

Ivan is now angry.

Philip continues:
Nor do I recognize the Tsar of the Orthodox
in heathen deeds.

The Tsar's Men have moved nearer to Philip.
Ivan, panting with rage,
halts the Tsar's Men.
He says angrily:
What business of thine, Black One,
are our Royal deeds?

Thy deeds are those of a bloodthirsty beast!

Silence, Philip! Do not oppose our power.
Else my wrath strike you!

The youths one by one stop in confusion;
as three they had repeated:
   Now a miracle shalt thou see.
   There shall be cast down . . .
Shadrach falls silent.
Meshach and Abednego continue:
   The Lord of Earth . . .
Meshach falls silent.
Abednego—the highest-pitched—on his own
in crystal tone has echoed:
   By the Lord of Heaven . . .

Amen!—the Chaldeans have spat out.
And crawled terrified underneath the furnace . . .

A movement among the people.

From the height of the ambo
Philip falls upon Ivan:
Like Nebuchadnezzar, Ivan, you burn
your nearest in the fire.
But, even as for his victims, there shalt come down an Angel with a
                                                                    sword
and lead them out of the pit.

He raises his hand toward the dome:
there, from a hook from which a luster has been removed,
there dangles on a rope a huge
parchment angel . . .

The end of the rope is held onto for dear life
by two monks.
They are frozen with fright
they look downward.

Bow to the Church, Ivan, and submit!
Abolish the Tsar's Men.
Ere the latest hour shall have passed!

A tremor has passed among the Tsar's Men:
hey, what if the Tsar were to agree! . . .

Tensely watch
Malyuta and the older Basmanov.

Fyodor is ready to hurl himself at Philip.

But Ivan shouts:
Silence, Philip!

He has sprung forward angrily at Philip.
The Tsar's Men with him.
The Tsar is on the verge of striking Philip a blow.

The boyars have frozen motionless with horror.

Abruptly in the complete silence
is heard the childish voice of the little boy:
Mummy! Is that the terrible Tsar of the Heathens?

Vladimir Staritsky has almost smirked . . .

Ivan has looked round . . .
A spasm has passed across his features . . .
Ivan has caught the smile on Vladimir's face.
As though with his glance he has snatched that smile:

the smile has disappeared from the face of Vladimir . . .

Ivan has transferred his glance to Euphrosyne:

Euphrosyne has shuddered,
has dropped her eyes . . .

Ivan has turned back sharply:
Henceforward I shall be such
as you name me!
He has rapped with his staff.

Euphrosyne has recoiled.

The monks have become bewildered.
They have let go the end of the rope.
Impetuously from the dome
hurtles down the gigantic angel.

The choir has burst out singing in triumph:
> *From death He saves.*
> *From the flames He delivers.*
> *The Tsar He rejects,*
> *And brings to naught* . . .
The angel falls on the furnace.
From under the furnace billow tongues of flame.
Some of the worshipers fall on their knees;
the Chaldeans prostrate themselves.

In the surrounding fire stands Ivan:
> *"Terrible" I'll be!*

FADE IN

AT THE STARITSKYS'

They've arrested Philip!—cries Euphrosyne Staritsky,
not yet recovered from the glance of the Tsar,
rushing in to the boyars.

The boyars are dumbfounded.
Vladimir Staritsky adds:

They wouldn't let him go back to the monastery:
he is to be tried by a savage court.
Tried!

Old man Peninsky says with a sigh:
Eigho, if, as in the old days, he were to be judged by a boyar court,
Philip would not be surrendered to insult.

EUPHROSYNE:
Recollect not the old—
to seek a way out is what's needful!

There's no way out!
'Tis ruin for all!

Says Euphrosyne:
There is a way out!

All are suddenly alert.
One way out. The last: kill the Tsar!

General panic. Confusion.

Vladimir Staritsky stammering,
frightened, tries to object.

Euphrosyne feels that there is no choice.
She says:
Either kill the Tsar.
Or lay our own heads on the block.

All are dumbfounded. Especially Funikov.

But someone's voice asks:
Who will do the killing? . . .

Again everyone is at a loss. Each is afraid.

Then rises the old man Pimen—the Bishop of Novgorod.
He has been sitting to one side. Now he speaks:
Only the pure in heart is fit for such a deed . . .
He indicates his novice, Peter.

The latter in fear falls on his knees.
While Pimen silently blesses him for the deed.

Euphrosyne places into his trembling hands a knife.
Vladimir Staritsky turns away frightened.

All go off hurriedly.

Euphrosyne goes up to Pimen.
Pimen says:
He has encroached on the lands of the Church.
We shall exterminate the beast!

EUPHROSYNE:
We ought to save Philip.
For us he took upon himself the wrath of Ivan.

Answers Pimen of Novgorod:
That depends upon who, in court, sits in judgment
over Philip . . .

Euphrosyne inquires anxiously:
Who will be chief judge?
To whom must be sent gold, furs, vessels?

Answers Pimen shortly:
I shall be chief judge . . .

Euphrosyne exclaims joyfully:
That means—he is safe!

But the answer falls, heavy as lead:
That means he will perish . . .

Euphrosyne is bewildered.
She looks questioningly.

Pimen explains:
Our cause needs Philip as a martyr:

a dead martyr, sainted, will inspire more dread for purposes of
struggle . . .

He shields Euphrosyne with the sign of the cross:
As a dead saint, even the Tsar shall not overcome him . . .

In his vestments white,
Within his eyes the dark flame of a fanatic,
Pimen exits from the gallery.

Euphrosyne straightens from her bow.
She stands as though struck by a thunderbolt.
Such savage malice,
such two-faced evil,
such theological craftiness,
even she, Euphrosyne, had never dreamed . . .

In silence Euphrosyne gazes after the holy man,
white as the moon, gray-haired;

white to the sight,
black and crafty in the soul . . .

Abruptly,
breaking Euphrosyne's silence,
Vladimir rushes to his mother.

Horrified, frightened of murder, he whispers:
Why are you pushing me to power?

The strong old woman takes her son in her arms.
Vladimir nestles to his mother like a child.

The mother soothes her son.
To her son she sings a lullaby.
A lullaby, strange, evil:

> *In the river,*
> *In the muddy little river,*
> *In Moscow river*
> *Bathed a beaver, a black beaver.*
>
> *The more he bathed—the more he muddied.*
>
> *After bathing, the beaver up the mountain climbed,*
> *Up the so high mountain,*
> *Looked around, peered around:*
> *Is there anyone coming? Anyone seeking?*
>
> *Hunters whistle, the black beaver seeking.*
> *Hunters trail, the black beaver stalking.*
> *They want to kill the beaver, they want to skin him.*
> *To sew a fox mantle, with black beaver trimmings,*
> *As a gift for Tsar Vladimir . . .*

With a howl of horror
Vladimir has recoiled from his mother.
He has cringed in a distant, tall, carved chair.

Euphrosyne rises from her bench after him;
she falls on her knees before her son.
She clasps his feet.

Says:
I am ready to bear you anew one hundred times in torment.
If but to raise you to the throne,
to see you on the throne . . .

Vladimir Staritsky has heard . . .
But Vladimir fears blood:
. . . blood is terrifying . . .

His mother soothes him.
She presses him to her breast like a little baby:
. . . You won't have to kill—Peter shall kill . . .
But Vladimir Staritsky is afraid:
And then, all one's life to be condemned:
to have him before one's eyes.
Ever the sight of him,
his look,
reproaching . . .

Having noiselessly opened the door:
Pimen's acolyte,
Peter, has entered . . .

Vladimir hides his head in fright:
terrified by the sight of Peter,
he presses against his mother.

Peter passes slowly toward the far corner.

Bending above her son,
the old woman whispers into Vladimir's ear,
keeping one eye on Peter in the distance:
Whatever happens, you yourself have nothing to fear:
when you ascend the throne,
as first task
the Tsar-killer you'll execute . . .

Peter has sat down on a bench . . .

And not him alone . . .

As if stung,
Vladimir tears himself from the embrace of his mother.
As though burned, he runs away from his chair.
His breathing comes heavily.
He hides his head:
he does not want to hear her terrible words.

But her serpent words sound from the distance:
A ruler must not swerve from the path of goodness,
if this may be,
but he must tread even the path of evil,
if this be inescapable . . .

She moves toward her son.

Again her son has almost dashed away:
but he stops short.

Once more the door has opened.
The empty space illumines. Peter has jumped up.

In the doorway—Malyuta.

Vladimir has shuddered.
Euphrosyne has flung herself towards him.
She has stood between Vladimir and Malyuta.
Has covered Vladimir with her body.
Has hugged him.
Has become motionless as stone.

But Malyuta is not menacing—
he is even humble in his attitude,
like a beaten cur.

Modestly he bows low. Respectfully.
He says to Euphrosyne:
Our great Sovereign confers upon you
a cup of wine . . .
To Euphrosyne a cup,
covered by a silken kerchief, he proffers.

Yet lower he bows to Vladimir:
And to his cousin—
Vladimir Staritsky—
our great Sovereign to the royal board
bids welcome . . .

Euphrosyne and Vladimir stand stupefied.

Malyuta looks at Peter with curiosity.

But suddenly the old woman's eyes light up with fire.
She whispers in her son's ear:
The finger of God!
Our cause—prospers . . .

She adds aloud, gladsomely,
as though delighted by the grace of the Tsar:
. . . *Take Peter along with you to the feast* . . .
She kisses her son upon the forehead.

Exeunt through the doorway:
Peter,

Vladimir Staritsky,
Malyuta—behind.

After them Euphrosyne to Vladimir
solicitously cries:
. . . *And don't forget to put on your new robe!*
She laughs at the double meaning of these words . . .

She has been left alone, contented.
She has fixed her gaze on the cup.

She has removed the kerchief.
Beneath the kerchief—a gold cup:

EMPTY . . .

Its bottom gleams gold.
Its reflection on Euphrosyne's face is gold.

Euphrosyne has marveled.
Has turned round the cup:
has recognized it!

It is that cup from which Anastasia before her death
received the poison.

The old woman has shuddered.
She has understood.
Far into the corner she has flung the cup.
She has taken hold of herself:
Who shall conquer whom, Tsar Ivan?
You—me?
Or the knife—you!

She has suddenly remembered:
Vladimir!—she has cried.

Rushed this way and that through the hall.
Snatched up the kerchief.
Put it on.

Quickly run out.

FADE OUT

FADE IN

A HALL

A clatter of dishes.
Banging. Hubbub.
Shouts:
Holla! Holla!

Forty martyrs look down from the low arched ceiling.
Their golden halos twinkle.

The feast is in full swing.
Black tunics are wildly dancing.
In their midst—a girl in a sarafan.
The Tsar's Men swig.
Shout:
Holla! Holla!

The Tsar's feast is in full swing.
The Tsar's Men swig. Shout.
And the Tsar shouts too:
Holla! Holla!

The girl twirls like a top.
The girl's face is covered by a mask,
painted in colors:
beneath her tiara—
fair plaits,
slant eyes.
Face white.
Rosy circles on the cheeks.

In the midst of the Tsar's Men are lost the "Lands' Men,"
the poor relations among them huddle in the corners . . .

At a table apart—Tartar princes and their suite.
Special honor is paid them:
they receive dishes from the Tsar's own table.

Along the walls a row of retainers.
Amidst them—Peter the Novice.
He sits like a black crow among the white servants.
His black satin shirt marks him out.

Beside the Tsar's seat—Vladimir Staritsky.
Ivan pours wine for him.
Affectionately getting him drunk.
Vladimir Staritsky has become considerably tipsy.
Tipsiness makes him benign.

Tsar's Men whirl dancing.
Among them—the girl in the sarafan.
Her mask smiles a dead, rapacious smile.
It recalls a grinning dog's head . . .

In contrast to this white face,
motionless amid the dance,
yet more frenzied appears the furious dance,
yet blacker the black tunics.

Beside the Tsar's seat—Vladimir Staritsky.
The Tsar affectionately plays with his curls.

Tsar Ivan has drunk much, but remains completely sober.
And beneath the shouting and the dancing he bends over Staritsky:
Eigho, thou dost not love me, Vladimir my brother . . .
Thou hast in thee no love for me, the lonely one . . .
I'm a poor forsaken orphan, and no one pities me . . .

The elder Basmanov's fist has banged on the table:
'Tis not fitting for the Tsar to hobnob with a Lands' Man,
least of all with a Staritsky!

Tsar Ivan will not suffer this rebuke to his royal conduct.
In violent anger he bursts out:
'Tis not for thee, Alyoshka, to teach the Tsar.
'Tis not for thee to raise a hand against the Tsar's kin!

But Basmanov replies:
But did you not teach us to uproot our kinship even as an oak tree?

The Tsar retorts:
Royal kin is a kin of kins.
And like not to any earthly oak,
but to the Tamarind Tree of Heaven.

But Basmanov is still not satisfied:
But are we not a new forest growing up around you?

The Tsar continues:
Oak shall not be destroyed to clear a place
for miserable ash.
Touch not the kin royal;
respect nearness to the Tsar in blood as holy!

But are we not closer to you—
by other,
poured-out,
blood more closely bound? . . .

But the Tsar lets fall in answer:
No kin art thou to me.
Thou art to me a bondsman.
From the dung I raised thee
to trample boyar traitors.
Through thee my will to realize.
Not to teach—but to serve—is thy bondsman's business.
Know thy place, Basmanov!
The Tsar vexes Basmanov.

Malyuta grins:
You are sick with a boyar vice, Alyoshka . . .
Place hunting.
You're green with envy: you'd like yourself to sit at the Tsar's right hand.

Angrily he has shaken his gray mane, the lionlike father Basmanov:
I swore a sacred oath: with boyars and Lands' Men not to keep company!

With a sharp turn he has risen from the board.
With a clatter passed through the rows of feasters.

Going out through the dance.
The dancers have become yet more frenzied, noticing the wrath of
Basmanov.

The sarafan has gyrated. Soared. As though parted from the earth.
Whirled through the hall like a hurricane.
Twirled beside the Tsar's seat like a top.
Stopped with an abrupt break.
Beads aside.
Plaits aside.
From under the mask—black curls.
From under the brows—familiar eyes.
From under the sarafan—a familiar frame.

The Tsar loves to amuse himself.
He loves to dress people up.
Masks—make entertainment.
So, see how Fedka entertains the Tsar with a dance, after dressing up in
costume.

Fedka hears the Tsar's words:
I'm a forsaken orphan, and no one pities me . . .
Umbrage seizes Fyodor.
Jealousy takes hold of the Basmanov:
surely this does not mean that Ivan
is ready to exchange Tsar's Men for kinsfolk.
And Fedka's eyes blaze in alarm.

Through half-closed eyes Ivan has given him a look.
He has winked.

The Basmanov has been pacified.
He has understood that the Tsar is playing a game.
He has whirled like a top more than ever.
Louder than ever the shouts: *Holla! Holla!*

Fedka bursts forth in song:
> *Guests have gone to the boyars' courtyards,*
> *Axes with the boyars are making gay* . . .
Wildly dance the Tsar's Men:
> *Holla, holla!*
> *Speak, speak!*

Speak and sentence 'em,
Speak and sentence 'em!
Fyodor:
With axes settle 'em!
A piercing whistle.

The Tsar's Men:
Hoy, burn, burn, burn! . . .

Alexey Basmanov has spat.
Has gone out sullenly through the doorway.

Louder than ever the shouts: *Holla! Holla!*
More frenzied than ever the noise and the dance.

More explosive than ever Fedka's song bursts:
The gates have split asunder,
Gold goblets go from hand to hand.
More wildly than ever dance the Tsar's Men.
Holla, Holla!
Speak, speak!
Speak and sentence 'em,
Speak and sentence 'em!
Fyodor:
With axes settle 'em!
A piercing whistle.

The Tsar's Men:
Hoy, burn, burn, burn! . . .
And beneath the dancing and the chorus, in drunken blabber,
Vladimir Staritsky assures the Tsar:
Hey, it's not true; you're Tsar of all Rus . . .
You've got friends . . .
And, wholly tipsy, he babbles disjointedly.

Ivan in merry mood plays up to the drunken speeches:
The conversation sounds like cross talk:
Not a friend in the world!
Oh, you have!

Well, who then?
What about me?

Eigh, I don't believe you!
Swear by God it's true!

Don't swear—prove it to me!
I'll prove it all right.

Artfully Fedka sings low:
> *When the guests from their revel left for home,*
> *The mansion behind them was burned to the bone.*
Comprehending, with lowered voices the Tsar's Men sing:
> *Holla, holla!*
> *Speak, speak!*
> *Speak and sentence 'em,*
> *Speak and sentence 'em!*
Deliberately this time Fyodor says:
With axes settle 'em!

A wild piercing whistle.
The Tsar's Men bellow with the full force of their lungs.
> *Hey, burn, burn, burn!*
Fyodor has finished his dance.
He has jumped on a bench.

With cries they swarm to embrace the dancer.
The tipsy bang their cups.
The sarafan costume is torn to pieces.

And Fyodor gleams in a dazzling white tunic,
pearl-embroidered.
He bursts into resounding laughter.
Praises, raptures shower and delight him.

Suddenly the smile disappears from his lips.
His glance has lit on the corner: stopped on Peter.
He has knitted his brows.

And asked abruptly of the servant Demyan:
Why amongst the servitors is this outsider—
Bishop Pimen's novice?

The servant explains to Fyodor:
Pimen lately assigned him
to the retinue of Vladimir Staritsky . . .

The young Basmanov has heeded, has shaken his head,
and looks earnestly in the direction of the Tsar.
He indicates Peter to the Tsar with his eye.

But Ivan continues as before, seeming to jest,
teasing the tipsy Vladimir:

You won't prove it—you're fibbing!
I will prove it—it's not a fib!

    Holla, holla!

The din becomes piercing:
Roast swans are borne in on platters.
Swans not white—
but black.

The gold dishes float by:
like black swans
they float by through the air above Vladimir.

Foremost the very biggest,
ornamented with a crown.

And Vladimir, in a sly tipsy whisper,
cunningly smiling,
blurts out to the Tsar:
Look how you're feasting and don't realize they want to get rid of you.

You don't say!
Honest to God!

But whomever will they put in my place?
Ah, you'll never guess!

Vladimir's stupid face smiles still more cunningly:

194

Vladimir, toward the swan on the dish—the black crowned one—
reaches.
His arm has brushed against a saltcellar.
Has upset it.

The salt has been spilled . . .

Those sitting nearby have grown numb;
they fear it as an evil omen.
Peter Volynets has risen from his place in the distance.
He has gone out through a small doorway . . .

Only Fyodor and Ivan have noted his exit.
They have exchanged glances.

The Tsar stands the saltcellar up again.

He goes on feasting.

Carefully, with his own hand,
to Vladimir from his cup,
he gives wine to drink . . .

Vladimir Staritsky babbles to himself:
Look, that's what I keep telling her; what's the fun in being a Tsar?
Plots, executions.
While I'm a peaceable fellow:
all I want is to fill a mug and sit in the corner . . .

Ivan has become reflective at the words "what's the fun . . ."
Reflectively he says:
True, true, what's the fun in being a Tsar?
Hard work—the Tsar's job.
Heavy work, the Tsar's.

Vladimir Staritsky is quite fuddled.
He continues captiously.
Grumbles under his breath:
Look, that's what I keep telling her; what good is it to me . . .
But she keeps nagging:
take it, wear the Royal cap,
take it, wear the Royal robe . . .

To Vladimir's words Ivan has long been attentively listening.
But he acts as though he were thoughtlessly repeating the words:
Wear the cap . . . wear the robe . . . wear . . .

Unexpectedly he shouts:
Wear them!
Brother o' mine! Why, indeed, why should'st thou not wear them?
Wear them, brother o'mine!

And right away, as though embarking on a jest,
the Tsar claps his hands.

196

Everything comes to a standstill . . .

The Tsar loves dressing up.
The Tsar loves dressing up other people . . .
He bids: *Bring here the Royal regalia!*

Malyuta and Basmanov adorn the guest
with the regalia of the Tsar.
They exchange winks.

Ivan himself seats Vladimir in the place of the Tsar.
He bends the knee to him.

All bend the knee to Vladimir Staritsky.

And this scene appears as a parody of that
in the prologue
when on the throne
sat the boy Ivan . . .

Vladimir Staritsky is confused and embarrassed.
All bow to him.

But at this very moment the throne begins to work:
the fool on the throne enjoys sitting there.
From the throne the fool smiles sweetly.
He seats himself more comfortably.

Ivan is watching Vladimir from the floor.
He sees him smile.
He reads his secret thoughts.
His eyes darken . . .

A far peal of bells rings out for matins.

From the floor Fedka has looked at Ivan.
Ivan on the floor has caught his look.
He has straightened up.
He has risen.
An end to jesting!

He calls to halt feasting.
He summons to prayer.

He exclaims:
Abandon this ungodly revelry!
And all is instantly transformed
to a monastic tone.

We summon thee, brethren, to the Lord!

Everyone has donned a black cassock.

Fyodor attires Ivan in the costume of an abbot;
he has dressed him in a black mantle . . .
He has given him a black cowl.

Let us remember the hour of death!
Ivan has donned the cowl.

The shameless songs have stopped short:
lighted candles are passing from hand to hand . . .

Alone on the floor—
with a dead smile—
Fedka's mask
smiles.

Ivan bids Vladimir:
Lead on to the Cathedral!
Vladimir Staritsky in full Royal raiment leads.

Near a small door, at the exit,
Vladimir Staritsky comes to a standstill.
The tipsiness is leaving him.
He desires to go no further . . .

But Ivan says to him admonishingly:
It is not becoming for a Tsar to hold back.
It is a Tsar's duty ever to go first . . .

He makes all bow to him, plead with him.

Vladimir Staritsky wants to get near Ivan.
He does not succeed.
He is obliged to go on.
He goes,
knowing what awaits him . . .

In the twilight, between the pillars at the left side of the Cathedral,
passes and disappears the figure of Peter . . .

Swaying, Vladimir Staritsky goes out through the doorway.
All follow him.

INSIDE THE CATHEDRAL

Through the twilight of the Cathedral moves the procession of Tsar's
Men.

In monkish cassocks.
Candle in hand.
With a muted chant:
> *Before God I swear*
> *A faithful oath,*
> *A weighty oath,*
> *A fearful oath.*
In front goes Vladimir Staritsky.

Peter's shadow has slipped between the pillars and hidden itself.

Vladimir Staritsky goes forward.
> *To serve the sovereign of Rus, like a dog:*
> *Its towns and villages to sweep with a broom,*
> *Villainous scoundrels to tear with my teeth,*
> *At the Tsar's command to lay down my bones*
> FOR THE SAKE OF THE GREAT RUSSIAN REALM . . .

Long is the way
between the Cathedral walls,
fresco-clad.
Terrifying is it to Vladimir.
His candle trembles in his hand.

To Vladimir the assassin seems to stand behind each pillar.
His agitation grows.
The interior of the Cathedral grows ever more dim.
The candles and dull chant of the Tsar's Men are in the distance.
The singing reverberates hollowly beneath the arches.
> *Before God I swear*
> *A weighty oath,*
> *To execute throughout Rus the will of the Tsar,*
> *To destroy throughout Rus savage robbers,*
> *To shed throughout Rus the blood of the guilty . . .*

Vladimir Staritsky advances.
The choir advances.
Vladimir Staritsky advances.
> *To burn out treason with fire,*
> *To cut out treachery with the sword . . .*

Beneath the arches at a small doorway in the darkness stands
Peter.
In his hand gleams a knife.
> *Not self nor others sparing,*
> FOR THE SAKE OF THE GREAT RUSSIAN REALM! . . .

Vladimir Staritsky advances.

Peter stands still.

The Tsar's Men sing:
>   *If I should break this fearful oath,*
>   *Then may my brother Tsar's Men pierce me*
>   *Mercilessly with their sharp daggers . . .*
Behind one of the pillars has flitted for an instant the shadow of
                                                        Malyuta.

Vladimir Staritsky has given a shudder
and turned to that side.

And, at that instant, Peter, with a sweep,
has plunged the knife between his shoulder blades.
>   *Then may I be overtaken by the penalty of death,*
>   *And by curses, and the tortures of Hell,*
>   *And by shame, and the torments of the damned . . .*
Vladimir Staritsky has crashed down to the stone floor on his face.
Peter has leaped away into the darkness of the doorway.
>   *Then may green mother earth reject me . . .*
The Tsar's Men stand rooted to the spot.

Through the Cathedral Euphrosyne comes running, triumphant.
She runs up to the body.
Places her foot on it.

She cries in triumph:
People, look!
Ivan is finished:
the beast is dead.
Rus shall bloom
beneath the sovereignty of a boyar Tsar
. . . Vladimir!

She has stopped suddenly.

The rows of Tsar's Men have made room.
And, from the depths, toward her, slowly . . .
advances Ivan.

Euphrosyne has given a shudder.
Peered down.
Bent over.
Turned the body over.
Recognized her son.
She has thrown herself on his bosom with a wail.

Peter, captured, is led up to Ivan.

Malyuta and Fedka are holding him;
they have twisted his hands tightly behind his back.
They are eager to tear him to pieces on the spot.
The rest of the Tsar's Men press threatingly around them.

Peter breathes heavily.
He twists in their grip.
Like a frantic beast he cries:
Execute me! Torture me!
I'll say nothing!
I'll name no one . . .

The ear of the Tsar catches these words.
He has moved towards Peter.
He comes close to Peter . . .

Peter stands stock-still . . .
The Tsar's Men have frozen . . .
Like ice.

But . . .
benign is the Tsar.
He chucks Peter affectionately beneath the chin.

Says to Malyuta and Fyodor:
Why are you holding him?
He has not killed the Tsar.
He has killed the fool.
Let him go . . .

Marveling, they let go of him.

Nor was it a fool he killed . . . he killed the Tsar's worst enemy.
I thank him . . .

And he embraces Peter.
All are dumbfounded.

Ivan takes a purse of money from his belt.
I grant a Royal gift—he gives him the purse.

Fedka, understanding nothing, stares at Ivan.

Ivan smiles with his eyes only, as though saying:
"Later you shall understand."

But her—he turns to Euphrosyne.

Above the body of her son she sits—a feeble,
grief-stricken,
helpless old woman . . .

HER . . .
he does not complete the sentence with the appropriate word:
"Arrest!"—
but silently has given the signal with his hand . . .

Malyuta's shadow comes over Euphrosyne.

Fedka is dragging away Vladimir's body by the feet.

Euphrosyne has screamed.

Singing, earnestly praying, the procession has moved onward.
> *May my fearful oath before God*
> *Be inviolable to the end of time,*
> *On earth and in Heaven alike,*
> F O R   T H E   S A K E   O F   T H E   G R E A T   R U S S I A N   R E A L M ! . . .
Ivan is in front.

The procession has become lost in the depths of the Cathedral.
> *. . . And may it stand for ages eternal,*
> *Inviolable for ever and ever.*
Peter is left alone.
He trembles. His teeth chatter.
> *. . . Amen! . .*
From the hands of Peter a few coins have fallen.
They have rung weakly on the stone . . .

FADE OUT

FADE IN

THE CASTLE OF WOLMAR

The heavy arches intersect one another with gray stones.
Like deadly enemies frozen forever in an embrace of stone.
A coat of arms, heavy, stone, is supported on the arches.
The coat of arms with mythological beasts
hangs above the Castle of Wolmar.

Below is heard a voice, speaking in a whisper.
The voice of Kurbsky, bent above a missive:
Truly, truly dost thou act, Ivan!
Without blood thou couldst not accomplish thy task . . .
Without blood thou couldst not build a State . . .

Savage beast—he suddenly grows infuriated:
Now even the very graves shall call
to Heaven for vengeance.
The stones cry out.
The heavenly trumpets shall raise their voices
for the saints thou hast tormented.
Write . . .
No, stop!

The young Italian scribe Ambrogio has stopped.
He has glanced up at the Prince with a questioning look.

Kurbsky says thoughtfully:
Truly dost thou act, Ivan.
On the throne I, too, would have acted so . . .

He grinds his teeth,
And why is it not I,

but thou, in glory there?
On the pathway to great deeds . . .

He has groaned:
While I . . .
I lie in the dust before the greatness of thy majesty.

The Prince lets himself sink down on a coffer of parchments.
A piercing husky wheeze comes from his breast.
Why not by these hands
are the great deeds wrought? . . .

He has shouted in despair:
Write:
Murderer, scum, offspring of Hell!

He does not himself believe in his savage words,
but cries furiously:
Write!
Thou art breeding in Moscow a pit of Hell!
Thou art drowning Rus in a sea of blood,
Thou art violating Russian soil! . . .

A *lie!*—he groans.
He adds in a whisper:
Thou art great, Ivan . . .

He has jumped over to Ambrogio.
Clutched tightly the narrow shoulders of the Italian.
Breathed hotly to him:
but not to him—to himself,
and not to himself but to all the world,
as though he had screwed himself up to reveal his inmost thought.
He speaks despairingly:
You must understand him, Ambrogio.
Things are not easy for him:
the load he bears is inhuman—
alone, deserted by his friends! . . .

He says, carried away by enthusiasm:
Amidst blood, he shines unprecedented . . .
Like Sabaoth above the waters, he hovers above a sea of blood:

and from that blood creates a firmament.
Out of that blood he forges works unprecedented:
he is building the realm of Rus . . .

Ambrogio raises his head wonderingly.
He asks Kurbsky:
If the Tsar of Muscovy be so great . . .
Why then, Prince Kurbsky, are you not by his side? . . .

The question has been pronounced barely audibly.
But with a thunderous horror
the words in the traitor prince's soul
evoke response,
as though the arches of Wolmar Castle
had crumbled within the Prince's heart:
Why? Myself I don't know!!
And he flings himself, collapsing, upon the wide couch.
His golden curls are buried in the cushions.

The heavy arches press tight together.
Intersecting one another.
Like deadly enemies,
frozen forever in an embrace of stone.
Under the arches hurried steps come running.
Prince!—cries Ambrogio.

Kurbsky lies motionless.

Prince!—cries Ambrogio.

Kurbsky's face lifts in a dull stare. His curls are tangled.

Prince!—cries Ambrogio.
A messenger from Moscow for you! . . .

The Prince springs up like an arrow from a bow.
He flings himself on Ambrogio:
It cannot be that the Tsar has forgiven me?
That he summons me to Moscow? . . .

Embracing Ambrogio,
like a steel blade

all taut—sprung,
he stands expectant.

On his breast glitters the Polish cross.

His brow is chill with sweat.
His features overlain with pallor.

Not an emissary from the Tsar—an emissary of Euphrosyne Staritsky—
the boyar Peninsky hurries in,
makes low obeisance to the Prince.

The Prince has given a shudder.
His eyes have gone dark.

He flings himself on the entering boyar like a wild beast.
Thou? . . . —he shouts.
With a Polish curse:
Dog's blood!
and then a Russian oath:
Hound of Hell!
he reviles the old boyar:
Lecherous dung!
The old man is thrown into a state of alarm . . .

The Prince cries:
Why so slow?
Thou wouldst be my ruin—
to shame me before my ally Sigismund?
Why does the revolt hang fire?
The rousing of the towns is overdue!
What is Pskov waiting for?
And—Novgorod?
The time is come to tear asunder
Ivan's Rus!

Stammering, Peninsky makes his excuses:
The towns are ready.
Pskov is prepared.
Novgorod is prepared.
All they lack is courage:
they tremble before the Tsar.
They fear chastisement . . .

This signal, then, shall fire them:
the moment the Tsar dares lift his hand against the free cities,
advances on Novgorod,
then throughout Rus shall resound the tocsin.
Rus, from end to end,
shall blaze with flames of insurrection!
Start thou, now instantly, for Lithuania!—

Kurbsky has beckoned another to him:
Henryk Staden! . . .

The German knight has appeared before him.
Avid lips. Blond hair.
Rusty armor.
Like a tattered eagle.
Face puffed with drink. Bags below the eyes.

Above the bags—the eyes.
Gray-blue. Piercing. Empty, cruel.

Ever in their cold gray seems to lurk
the hostility of the cold North Sea.

Henryk Staden is burly.
Bony.
Long, gripping arms.
The fists—covered with a ginger down.
Freckled.

Worm your way among the Tsar's Men . . .
Play the innocent.
Send news of the Tsar's armies . . .

he has taken out a purse of gold from a casket.
Has given it to Staden.

Has flown over to Ambrogio.
Cried out:
Write to Sigismund—'tis time to start!

FADE OUT

FADE IN

THE "TERRIBLE'S" LIBRARY

A door opens into a subterranean chamber.
Malyuta comes in quickly.
Behind him—Peter Volynets.

Around are many books.
Among them Cicero. Livy. Suetonius.

Fedka and Ivan's confessor—Eustace—are standing there.
Eustace, who does not look up, is turning the pages of Aristophanes.
O F F S C R E E N the voice of Ivan is dictating clearly:
*How is it, Kurbsky, that thou art not ashamed: to name villains
martyrs, without considering
why they fell victim* . . .

Staring gloomily in front of him, Ivan says:
*And shouldst not thou thyself, Kurbsky, then be
compared to Judas, the traitor?*

A pause. The scribe has stopped.

Not looking at anyone,
Ivan has moved over to his throne.
His gaze, dull-eyed, is fixed on one spot.

Peter flings himself on his knees before Ivan.
Malyuta whispers to Ivan:
He wants to talk . . .

Ivan has gazed from the throne at Peter.
Sharp attention has gleamed in his eyes.
It is evident that Ivan has waited for this coming.
This is evident from Fedka's delighted look at Ivan.
This is evident from the satisfied answering look of the Tsar.

Peter is sobbing meanwhile at the Tsar's feet.
He returns the money:
I am unworthy. I have not been open.
I have hidden the truth from the Tsar.
Execute me, Tsar, unworthy being that I am . . .

Ivan soothes him "like a loving father," tenderly:
Gives him water.
And hearkens with attention . . .

I'll tell all about the evil . . .
That deed of murder was the work not of one—but of three,
as the icon of the Mother of God is often—a triptych,
so in the murder was it—three hands were mingled . . .

Ivan bends forward . . .

One hand—beyond the border—roused me to treason.
Another hand—by his sermons gave me courage.
The third—placed in my hand the knife.

Ivan bends lower. He listens.

Kurbsky—was the first hand . . .

Ivan, in his distress, whispers aloud:
Andrew . . . Andrew . . . What did not suffice thee . . .
Or didst thou covet my Royal cap?

Peter continues:
Pimen—was the second hand!

Ivan has straightened on his throne:
Pimen—who, as chief judge, against Philip
called for the penalty of death?

Peter continues:
The name of the third hand—is that of Philip himself.
He was bound as one with Pimen in the deed.
In everything Pimen's instructions he fulfilled.
With his passionate speech in the Cathedral he persuaded me.

Ivan sits like a statue.
He has let his head fall crash onto the table.
He has groaned aloud:
Philip . . . Philip . . . my last friend, my old friend . . .

Peter continues:
This is but little.
In this plot with Pimen
are Pskov and Novgorod . . .

Malyuta has become alert. Fyodor has moved closer.
Eustace crosses himself.

Pskov and Novgorod,
with Pimen, voivodes* and boyars,
are breaking from Muscovy,
and joining the Livonian State.

A lie!—
Eustace cries angrily in a piercing voice.

The Tsar looks askance at Eustace.
A spark of suspicion flashes in the Tsar's eye.

Peter rejoins:
Confirmation exists in a document of agreement:
the plot of Pimen
with Kurbsky, with the Poles, with the Livonians
lies hid in the recesses of the Cathedral of St. Sophia,
behind the icon of the Mother of God . . . a triptych!

Struck to the very heart by the treachery of his friends,
his head supported on the table,
Ivan sits.
Barely audible, he whispers to Eustace:
What is to be done, Father?

Then with unexpected force
speaks the small and slight confessor:
Know no mercy!

* *Voivode*—a governor of a castle or other military post.

217

Punish Novgorod with fire and sword!

Peter is startled
to hear from this mild-seeming fellow
such fearful words.

But words yet more fearsome are to come.
Eustace cries out fanatically:
Like Judas Maccabeus,
like Joshua against the Philistines,
so let the Tsar march on a new Crusade,
against the modern Babylon—
against Novgorod! . . .

. . . *Make the earth to tremble.*
Shake the whole soil of Rus,
as it sees how a great Sovereign
goes to punish traitors!

Tears of conviction stand in Eustace's eyes.
Fedka has grasped his sword.
Peter is enthralled.

Only Malyuta looks doubtfully from beneath his brows.

Ivan embraces the confessor:
Yes, march against Novgorod . . .

A smile has slid across the face of Ivan.
But not with shouting and cymbals . . .
Mildly—
by a march in secret
we shall advance . . .

So that no one shall know . . .
So that no one—
nor man,
nor beast,
nor bird—
shall convey unto the rebel town
report that, like a tempest, on it moves
the wrathful Tsar . . .

Ivan continues:
Sever every link with Novgorod . . .
Malyuta watches understandingly.

Between us and the Livonians erect a screen . . .
Fyodor hurries off with the command.

The Tsar has stared at Eustace.
Your lot—to stay in Moscow.
Eustace is puzzled.

Ivan has narrowed his eyes with cunning:
Blessed is he who takes no part in the counsel of deceitful men.
Yet more:
it is not fitting for the righteous
to be present at the committing of a sin.
Else, how afterward as a confessor
could he condemn that sin?

With wide-open eyes
Eustace stares after the Tsar.

His radiant eyes vanish in darkness.

AND ALREADY THERE FADES IN
A S N O W Y P L A I N

Across a snowy plain skis are soundlessly gliding.
Skis are gliding across the snow.
Advancing across the snow on ski are detachments
of Tsar's-Men foot.

Following them are horse.
Among the horse—the Tsar.

Behind—the wrecks of houses, heaped with snow.
On the snow—sabred bodies.

The skiers glide over the snow . . .

At an outpost, on patrol duty—Novgorod warriors.

The skiers have approached them soundlessly.

Bows have bent. Arrows soared.

The Novgorod patrols have fallen in the snow.

"So that no one—
nor man,
nor beast,
nor bird—
shall convey unto the rebel town
report that, like a tempest, on it moves
the wrathful Tsar . . ."

The Tsar's Men move on skis over the snow . . .
On the snow lie bodies,
transfixed by arrows and cut down by swords.
Slaughtered cattle.

A dog has fled to one side;
it is struck by an arrow.
Yelping hoarsely, the dog has buried its muzzle in the snow.

In silence the Tsar's army glides over the snow.
Among the Tsar's Men—a new face.
The German, Staden, moves over the snow.
Attentively he watches everything.

Arrows shoot down the birds of the sky,
". . . so that no one—
nor man,
nor beast,
nor bird—
shall convey unto the rebel town
report that, like a tempest, on it moves
the wrathful Tsar . . ."

Skis glide over the snow . . .

The Tsar is gloomy.
The treachery of Philip weighs heavy on him.

He summons Malyuta.
Entrusts him with an errand:
. . . *To Tver Novices' Cloister, hurry* . . .

Ivan rides on gloomily against the background of the snowy plain.

Far ahead
advances the vanguard.

Suddenly the far-off vanguard has noticed,
outstripping them,
someone ahead
along gullies
hastening.

The skis have dashed forward.
The vanguard has surged forward.

But the fellow takes to his heels.

The Tsar's Men have pursued him.
Chased him silently—
to give tongue they are forbidden.

Bows have bent.

Three arrows have hit the runaway.

The ski cavalcade of Tsar's Men moves onward . . .

The runaway has turned over on the snow.

He has pulled a message out of his cap.
Brought it to his mouth.
Torn a piece off it with his teeth.

At that moment the vanguard has come up with him.
Has snatched away the message.

Fedka Basmanov has come up.
But could learn nothing—
the runaway is dead.

The German Tsar's Man rides on;
observantly he watches everything . . .

The Tsar's Men ride on, move ahead on skis.
The skis glide over the snow.

The Tsar is gloomy.

Behind him, Malyuta is downcast.

The vanguard flies up to the Tsar on ski.
Fyodor hands the message to the Tsar,
says in a whisper:
From Moscow—a report to Novgorod,
that the Tsar of Muscovy has set forth against it . . .
But where the signature should be
is torn away . . .

The Tsar has contracted his brows.
Crushed the message in his fist.
Flung it aside.
And bidden the advance move faster.

Nearby is Novgorod—the rebel city.
Behind the Tsar—the snowy waste.

Covered with snow lies the Moscow messenger.
Protruding from him are the three arrows . . .
                                        FADE OUT

NOVGOROD.   DAWN

The great hall of Pimen's palace.
The huge space is weakly illuminated.

Pimen is with a group of Novgorod boyars and voivodes.
Among them—the boyar Peninsky, recently at Kurbsky's.

Pimen of Novgorod is unrecognizable.
A dark flame blazes beneath his white chasuble.
His warlike countenance breathes a cold ecstasy.

The body, emaciated, feeble, seems to gather vigor;
it seethes with a victorious tremor;
the aim of his life is attained.
He has lived to see the fulfillment of his works.
He revels in the foretaste of victory.
He fierily declares:
The hour has struck!
Beneath the banner of the cross, we go to battle.
We'll rouse Pskov and Novgorod.
Pskov and Novgorod shall lead the remaining towns.
A message has come from Kurbsky:
all is ready for the invasion,
we want no more to be with Moscow.
From Moscow we secede—
to the Livonian State we shall adhere!

He comes up closer to his confidants:
In Moscow I have—trusted men:
spies.
Should Ivan think to move on Novgorod:
from village to village,
from outpost to outpost,
like fire,
like the birds of the air,
like the tempestuous wind,
the news would fly:
with arms in hand, to meet
the Tsar, would go Pskov and Novgorod . . .

He has sat down:
From hour to hour I await a messenger from Moscow.
Sent by a true man,
close to the Tsar,
by name . . .

He has opened his mouth to name the name—
has choked . . .
He does not believe his eyes:
facing him in the doorway
Tsar Ivan stands.
Behind the Tsar, Malyuta.
The Basmanovs.
The Tsar's Men.

The voivodes and boyars of Novgorod are struck numb.
The curt order has rung out:
ARREST HIM!

The wrathful countenance of Ivan retreats into darkness.

FADE IN
A CORNER WITHIN THE CATHEDRAL

The angry countenance of the Tsar of Heaven,
Sabaoth,
in a fresco of the Last Judgment.

The Tsar of Heaven is holding the last Judgment:
he is calling the righteous to himself,
casting sinners into fiery Gehenna.

From the choir a monk intones:
> *Have mercy, O Lord, on the deceased,*
> *Thy servants male and female,*
> *On those who have gone to rest before their time*
> *From Adam and unto this very day . . .*

Around the Heavenly Tsar
are ranged fiery circles:
the hierarchy of Heaven painted.
Fiery swords are directed downward
by the winged Tsar's Men of the Tsar of Heaven.
Down,
thither, where, in eternal flames
sinners are burned by eternal fires.
The voice of the monk is heard:
> *Have mercy, O Lord,*
> *On God's servant Vladimir Prince Staritsky . . .*

The silhouette of the monk grows out of the darkness:
> *Have mercy, O Lord,*
> *On Inokina, Princess Eudoxia,*
> *Known in the world as Euphrosyne Staritsky,*
> *To whom it befell to drown in the river Shaxna . . .*

The monk has finished intoning from one scroll.
He unrolls a new obituary list:

> *Have mercy, O Lord,*
> *On the souls of Thy servants*
> *of Novgorod . . .*

The melancholy enumeration of the names extends.
The obituary list unrolls in an endless scroll.

> *Have mercy, O Lord, on the most saintly*
> *Pimen, Prelate of Novgorod,*
> *Known in the world as Prokopy Cherny.*
> *Kazarin and two sons.*
> *Ishuk. Bogdan. Iohannis. Iohanna.*
> *Ignaty. Grigory. Fyodor.*
> *Istom . . . Prince Vasily . . .*

In the darkness below the fresco of the Last Judgment
in a corner,
where most insatiably of all
the eternal fires devour sinners,
lies prostrate
Tsar Ivan.

Some distance behind him, in the background, stands
Malyuta.
The Basmanovs:
father and son.
In shadow: the German Tsar's Man, Staden.

Not all the names of the slain are known, and this is why
from time to time
the enumeration is interrupted by the words:

> *The names also of these, Thou, O Lord, shalt reckon . . .*

The voice of the monk comes from above Ivan:

> *. . . Bakhmet. Ioannis. Bogdan.*
> *Michael. Tryphon. Artemy.*
> *Twenty people of Ivanov.*
> *The names also of these, Thou, O Lord, shalt reckon . . .*

Prostrate in the dust lies Tsar Ivan.
Above him hangs the Last Judgment.
On a throne above the Tsars sits the Heavenly Judge.
The eyes of Sabaoth flash lightning.
And his face is dark with wrath . . .

At his feet the sinners burn in eternal fire.

But, more fearfully than hellfire, remorse
tortures, scorches, gnaws
at the soul of the Tsar of Earth—
of Muscovy.
He accounts as his a fearful responsibility.
Sweat pours in streams from his forehead.
Scorching tears stream from his closed eyes.
The Tsar has grown thin, emaciated.
And seems yet older by a dozen years.

The monk intones:
> *Prince Peter,*
> *Nicephorus and wife and two sons.*
> *Simeon and wife and three daughters.*
> *Chizh, with wife and son and daughter.*
> *Sumorok. Okhlop. Nechay.*

Malyuta tells the younger Basmanov:
In all were executed in Novgorod
one thousand five hundred and five souls . . .
And Ivan's lips whisper,
as though he were justifying the terrible deed:
Not from malice. Not from wrath. Not from savagery. For treason.
For betrayal of the cause of the whole people . . .

He awaits an answer from Sabaoth.
But the wall is silent.

Clearly sounds the obituary role:
> *Anna. Irene. Alexis. Agatha. Xenia.*
> *Her two sons. Isaac. Zachary's two daughters.*
> *Glyceria. Eudoxia. Mary.*
> *Fifteen women slain in Novgorod.*
> *The names also of these, Thou, O Lord, shalt reckon* . . .

Malyuta tells the elder Basmanov:
Monasteries pillaged and destroyed number one hundred and seventy . . .

And Ivan hastens to offer explanation of the bloody deed:
Not for self. Not for greed's sake. For the country. Not from savagery.
But to safeguard the land.

And he gazes entreatingly into the eyes of the Dark Countenance.
But the eyes do not gaze down.
Their painted gaze is set in the far distance . . .

Clearly audible in the silence is the obituary roll:
 Dokuchay. Nicephorus. Callinicus. Parthenius.
 Prince Boris. Prince Vladimir.
 Andrew. Prince Nikita.
 Three clerks. And five serfs.
 The names also of these, Thou, O Lord, shalt reckon . . .
Says Ivan in anguish:
Thou art silent? . . .
He has waited. No answer.

Angrily, with defiance,
the Earthly Tsar to the Heavenly Tsar
has repeated threateningly:
Thou art silent, Tsar of Heaven?!

The Figure is silent.

Then flings, as a mighty gage,
the Earthly Tsar at the Heavenly Tsar
his jewel-studded staff.

The staff shatters on the smooth wall.
It smashes to splinters.
The scintillating stones fly through the air.
Scattered like Ivan's prayers, to Heaven addressed in vain . . .

And the Earthly Tsar sinks down,
crushed by the inexorability of the Tsar of Heaven.

Thou deignest no answer to the Tsar of Earth . . .
his strength forsaking him, beating himself against the wall, whispers
             Tsar Ivan.

But the stern, painted Sabaoth on the wall is silent,
seated on His great throne above the stars.

Around Him is silent the hierarchy of angels.
Are silent the sinners: they writhe in eternal fire.
>   *Alexis and wife. Vasily and wife.*
>   *Andrew and wife. Their son Lazarus.*
>   *Bogdan and wife.*
>   *Nezhdan and wife. Baloban and wife . . .*
Fyodor watches with anguish in his eyes.
Fyodor feels sympathy for the Tsar. He whispers:
Heavy is the task of a Tsar . . .

On the ground Ivan gives a hoarse rattle.
He is crushed.
Fire scorches his soul.
>   *Molchan. Vsyachin. Gryasnov.*
>   *Ivan. Polivov. Obernibesov.*
>   *A visiting scribe.*
>   *Nelyub . . .*
To Alexey Basmanov has come up his lieutenant—
Demyan, who once served among the Staritskys' bondsmen.
Gold treasures and icons from the Church of St. Theodore Stratilatos
in Novgorod—where should they be taken?
To the Palace of the Mint or . . .

To the Palace of the Mint. For the Treasury—Basmanov-father has inter-
>   rupted him.
And cast a glance in the direction of his son.

The eyes of Basmanov-son are filled with tears.
His gaze is fixed undeviatingly on Ivan.
He does not hear.
>   *Rop Nemchim. Litvin. Maxim.*
>   *The fisherman Korepan. The cook Moliva.*
>   *The fisherman Yozh. In Bolshoye Ivanov seventeen persons.*
>   *In Gorodishche*
>   *Three persons . . .*
>   *The names also of these, Thou, O Lord, shalt reckon . . .*

And Basmanov-father adds through his teeth to Demyan.
Take along a third of the baggage to the Basmanovs' place near Moscow:
no one being let know. As has always been taken . . .

229

By his side resounds a cheerful voice:
I'll buy the baggage!
Staden the German has approached.
I'll pay with sables.
Which, in Novgorod . . . I liberated!

He has looked up suddenly.
Fyodor is staring at him point-blank;
with eyes wide open
Fyodor is gazing at the German:
Cheating the Treasury?
Betraying the Tsar?

Your father Alexey
always disposes so . . .
Demyan tries to pass it off.

Fyodor has turned brusquely:
I shall go to the Tsar!

Demyan in panic squeezes against the wall.

Alexey Basmanov
has seized his son by the arm.

Pale, Staden has whispered through his teeth:
Give me away—you give away your father!

They face one another like wild beasts.
The breath of one comes straight up against the other's face.

To one side, Demyan trembles.

A heavy knocking interrupts them.
They see:
Tsar Ivan again and again beats his head in obeisance upon the ground.
He beats his forehead on the stone.
His eyes pour with blood.
Blood veils his sight.
His reason is clouded.
His eyes are darkened . . .

He has straightened his back, he sways.
Stretches out his arms. Grasps the air. Seeks support.
Pastor, pastor . . . —he whispers with a dry mouth.
He rises from his knees and stands erect.

Fyodor has dropped his eyes.
Averted his head.
Vanished behind a pillar.

Alexey reaches out after his son.
His hands are suspended in the air.
Staden smiles ironically.

Swaying, Ivan moves through the Cathedral.

As God's holy, he'll betray them to the Tsar!—
whispers Demyan to himself, his teeth chattering.
And, crossing himself, he ducks into the darkness of the Cathedral.

Past Staden and the Basmanovs,
seeing nobody,
Ivan passes . . .

With face of stone
Alexey gazes after Fyodor.

In his expression is not fear,
but anguish.
Anguish for his son,
to his father lost forever.

Staden slaps the veteran encouragingly on the back . . .

To confess . . . hoarse and dull croaks Ivan's voice.
And swaying, with infirm step, stumbling,
he has made his way into the darkness of the Cathedral
to the choir.
Past the impassive cantor.
Past the gilded "Tsar's Gates."
To a little door with an angel.

The door has squeaked softly in turning.

Who calls upon the Lord?—
resounds from the altar
the clear voice of Eustace.

His unworthy servant Ivan—
dully has echoed
from the stone floor . . .
          Have mercy, O Lord, on the souls of Thy servants,
          one thousand five hundred and five persons . . .
A heavy pause.

Silent, his head bowed,
stands Malyuta.
Fyodor beyond.
They are sad at the heavy lot of a Tsar . . .

Motionless, father Basmanov
gazes at his son.

The monk begins a new scroll:
> *Have mercy, O Lord, on the souls of Thy servants* . . .
> *Pimen—most holy Prelate*
> *of Novgorod,*
> *known in the world as Prokopy Cherny* . . .
Eustace has bent down over the Tsar.
He listens.

The voice of Ivan comes from under the stole.

His breast heaves in gasps.
His soul bursts out in a groan:
Heavy is it to build a State at such a price . . .
Bloody sweat runs down across his forehead.
He names names.
Beside him hovers suspended the cross of his confessor:
The most crafty treasonous brood of Kolychevs . . .

The confessor's cross has trembled.

Ivan names:
The Metropolitan of Moscow, Philip,
at Tver Novices' Cloister, strangled . . .

The face of the confessor has paled.
The angelic clarity of his eyes has changed to alarm.
He has whispered, repeating the name:
Philip . . .

The cross beside Ivan has been allowed to droop lower.

Ivan continues:
. . . of that unworthy Philip
the brothers:
Andrew,

Vasily,
Benedict . . .

In mortal fear,
the confessor asks:
And . . . Timothy?

Ivan has sharply raised his glance.
The question has surprised him.
He says:
. . . Being sought . . .

The confessor sighs deeply:
. . . And Michael?

Suspicion seizes Ivan.
He has contracted his brows.
He speaks with deliberation.
He will be captured.

The confessor has made an abrupt sideways movement.
He breathes heavily.

Ivan says:
The youngest, only, can nowise be discovered . . .

The confessor has gripped his cross more tightly.
Drawn it back close to his body.

Ivan and his confessor find themselves face to face:
It cannot be that thou thyself art of that unhallowed brood,
the junior of the Kolychev clan,
vanished without report?

He moves yet closer to the confessor:
It cannot be that thee,
the last,
Philip Kolychev hid:
masking the trail in the very jaws of the lion . . . ?

He absorbs Eustace with his eyes:
Nor also that by thee that message
to Novgorod was sent? . . .

Ivan grasps Eustace tightly by the cross.
His hands move along its chain.

Along the chain of the cross
to the throat of the confessor
they steal up.

And see, already the confessor is on his knees.
And, like a hawk, above him hovers Tsar Ivan.
Speak . . . speak . . .

The thin chain tightens on his neck.
The confessor begins to choke.
I'll tell all . . . he croaks.
He reaches up to the ear of the Tsar.

He whispers brokenly:
Kurbsky but waits the signal . . .
All outposts on the frontier
by the Livonian Ambassador have been bought . . .
Thy own boyars betray thee to the foe . . .

Tsar Ivan has flung Eustace from him.
In anger he has hid his face between his hands.

From the ground the confessor continues:
And, in that plot—
the Chancellor Mikita Funikov,
Prince Afanasy Vazemsky,
the voivodes of the Livonian outposts,
the princes
Lobanov, Bychkov, Khokholkov—
of Rostov . . .

Ivan has stepped toward Eustace
as a man steps about to tread on the head of a viper:
Now tell . . .
whom of these you have enmeshed by calumny? . . .

Neither alive, nor dead,
lies the confessor on the floor.

Malyuta springs up out of the darkness.
Eustace cowers.

ARREST HIM! . . .
MAKE HIM TALK! . . .
FORCE A CONFESSION! . . .

Malyuta seizes Eustace.

Ivan has removed his hands from his face.
His eyes shine with new vigor.
He has shouted loudly:
Fedka!

The young Basmanov has run up.
With savage gaiety Ivan has ordered:
A scribe hither!

The scribe has come running:
Write . . . to Kurbsky!

And Tsar Ivan has added, deliberately:
*And sign the missive
with the name . . .
of Eustace!*

FADE OUT

THE PALACE OF SIGISMUND

Ivan is in our hands!—
cries the excited Kurbsky, running in.

He straightens out on the table a missive
that has secretly arrived from Moscow.

Above it bend greedily
the representatives of the coalition
against the State of Muscovy.
Kurbsky points to a passage.
He explains:
The outposts on the Livonian frontier have been bought.
The way to Moscow is open.

Sigismund smiles wanly.
His gout has got worse after these years.
And one foot is crippled by that cruel illness.
His right arm is useless.
He cannot give the customary signal with his hand.
But the King's smile is sufficient—
all cry ecstatically:
Vivat!

For not one of those present can know
that this missive
suspiciously resembles
the one that Ivan started to dictate
in the preceding scene.

And that the missive has been signed falsely . . .
with the name of Eustace.

But a doubt suddenly seizes Sigismund.

Silently,
and with a tortured grimace,
he turns to one of his grandees.

And the grandee expresses the King's thought:
But England? . . .

Sigismund points with his left hand to another grandee
and that grandee utters the King's question.
The grandee: *Is there an alliance between Ivan of Muscovy*
and Queen Elizabeth? . . .

And the common thought is completed
by the merry, round-faced jester:
The King wants to know whether Ginger Bess
will kick us in the . . .

The jester smacks himself resoundingly on the bottom.
Jumps up on the middle of the table,
lowers his ponderous bottom
onto the map spread over the huge table.

And, seated somewhere at the approaches to Moscow—
between Lithuania and Livonia,
as between two stools—
the jester gives a cunning smile.
He negatively wags his head
and shakes his bells;
he takes up a lute
and begins to sing
''THE BALLAD OF GINGER BESS.''
   The King's lost his way in the gray, gray mist.
   He would seek out Britain's isle.
   A man shall go into the Queen's great house—
   And speak her cleverly . . .
Mandolins join in.

        FADE OUT

FADE IN
A curly-haired page sings in the embrasure
of a Tudor window:
   And only God in his high Heaven knows
   Whom Bess will take for the night,
   Whom next morn she'll give honey,
   Whom next morn she'll give wax,

Whom next morn she'll give a sting—
And everyone has his turn.
He says:

Ginger Bess . . .

And at that moment, on the screen:

A CORNER ROOM IN
WINDSOR CASTLE

A private audience in the apartments of Queen Elizabeth
of England.

The years have laid their imprint on the visage of the Virgin
Queen. Her dress has become yet more magnificent.
There is even more powder on her face.
And this makes her hair seem still more fiery-red.

Even more youthful is her current favorite,
half hidden behind the gold lace of her raiment.

Like a soldier on guard, stands, all in gold,
stiff to attention, before her Royal throne
the figure of the Queen.

In the shadow behind her—the current lover.
This—is not yet Essex. At this time Essex is still a child.
Maybe he—is Christopher Hutton, or Edward Vere.
But, most likely, it is young Charles Blount—
"A curly-headed boy with a perfect figure
and a delicate face, that blushed red
when the glance of Her Majesty
looked approvingly on him."

Facing the Queen, a secret emissary.
He is clad in severe attire.

And only by his round face do we recognize the man
who, under the mask of a jester, wrought the will
of the German Imperial Princes at the court of Sigismund.

Now the face is sweaty and tired.
The German wheezes, and coughs continuously.

Sings the page in the embrasure:
> *By day, by night, orates the man—*
> *He pledges scores of wonders.*
> *The man he sings, he wheezes on.*
> *Queen Bess she gives no sign . . .*

It is plain that the German's eloquence has lasted many hours.
His knees are giving way beneath him.
And, with superstitious awe, the German emissary gazes
at the rocklike immobility of the Queen
able to stand, without flinching,
through long hours of endless audiences . . .

Exhausting himself, for the tenth time
the German assures the Queen:
A coalition against Ivan is essential
so that England should untie our hands.

To the Germans it is essential that England
should not intervene in case of an attack on Muscovy.

The coalition is essential
so that England should aid the Germans . . .

The page sings:
> *And only God in his high Heaven knows . . .*

The German mops his face.
> *Who's bought and who's sold by Ginger Bess.*

Elizabeth gazes ahead of her with a far-off, glassy stare.
> *Whom next morn she'll give honey,*
> *Whom next morn she'll give wax,*
> *Whom next morn she'll give a sting . . .*

Sings the page in the embrasure:
> *And everyone has his turn,*
> *Ginger Bess . . .*

Young Blount is outlined, standing near the Royal throne.

A wearisome pause.

Mellowly twang the mandolins.

And at last the Queen lets fall the long-awaited assent:
ENGLISH MEN-AT-ARMS SHALL BE THERE, IN RUSSIA.

To be sure, like all the decisions of Elizabeth,
this decision too has been formulated to be highly significant and
                                                    ambiguous:
if one pleases, these words can be endowed with a meaning
exactly opposite to that
which the German wishes to hear in them.

But the completely exhausted emissary
is by now incapable of appraising the answer of the Queen.
He rejoices at her words.
And hastily removes through a small secret door.

The door slams,
and, with unexpected suddenness, there breaks in
a chorus of cavaliers in the courtyard—
outside the window of the small reception hall in Windsor Castle.
       So, high for Bess raise the icy draught.
       Drink up, merry men; beat on, waves of the sea!
Umph!—the German comes hurrying out onto the courtyard.

THE CHORUS:
       To our Good Queen Bess,
       To the devil's own Bess,
       To Ginger-curl Bess . . .
His strength forsakes the German.
His knees give way under him.
Someone's kindly hands prevent him from falling . . .

She's as artful and cunning as Old Nick,—
groans the German.

The glance of the emissary falls on the man
who lent him support:
before him is the Ambassador of Muscovy—
Osip Nepeya.

THE CHORUS:
       Good old Bess,
       Wise old Bess,

Shameless Bess,
Mighty Bess,
   Queen of the English Men.
The German pulls himself up arrogantly,
inflated with success.
Smiling ironically,
he goes out . . .

Ha-ha-ha—from behind the doorway is heard
the hearty soldier's laugh of Queen Bess.

Nepeya looks at the door anxiously.

But behind the door the motionless sphinx has come to life:
with a boyish gaiety Elizabeth completes a remark
she was addressing to the lad Blount:
As always—the German is ready to pay
with the skin of an unkilled bear.
And this time the bear's—a Russian one! . . .

Blount is puzzled.
But what about your answer, Majesty?

And, in reply to him,
herself trills
GINGER BESS:
   "And only God in his high Heaven knows:
   Who's bought and who's sold by Ginger Bess . . ."

Learn diplomacy! . . .
says the Queen.

In the embrasure of the window
sings the page:

> *Whom next morn she'll give a sting,*
> *Whom next morn she'll give wax,*
> *Whom next morn she'll give honey* . . .

The Queen takes the tender chin of Blount
between her long fingers.
> *. . . And everyone has his turn* . . .

The Queen pats Blount on the cheek.

THE PAGE:
> *Ginger Bess* . . .

The Queen throws herself down on the throne and roars with laughter.
Of all the merry wives of Windsor town,
you, Bess, are still by far the most dangerous!—
says Blount, kissing her hand.
The Queen roars with laughter.
It is hard to decide what Ginger Bess is laughing at—
at the German envoy,
at her own thoughts,
or at her lover's phrase,
which, by the end of her reign, will have become enshrined
in the title of an immortal comedy . . .

Most probable of all is it
that she's laughing at something entirely different.

The Queen looks at Blount.
Blount's tender face suffuses with a blush . . .

From the distance rises the twanging of the mandolins.
And—as though going away on tiptoe—
dies out the singing of the chorus:
> *Our Queen Bess* . . .
> *Ginger Bess* . . .
> *Shameless Bess* . . .
> *Queen of the English Men* . . .

The scene disappears into darkness.
The mandolins twang mellowly.

Suddenly they are interrupted by heavy blows on bronze.
One. Two. Three.

FADE OUT

THE LIVONIAN BORDER

The Outpost at Rotten Marsh.
Dusk.
A patrol.
One man on a tree,
another mounted—beneath the tree.

A guard-hut.
Inside the hut—the voivode.
Prince Lobanov-Rostovsky.
Suddenly there enters a group of Tsar's Men.
Malyuta at their head.
The voivode is arrested.

Through the darkness advances a Royal army.

Dusk.
A patrol.
One man on a tree,
another under the tree—on horseback.
And beyond, all happens identically,
save for this difference, that here
the voivode—
is Prince Bychkov-Rostovsky.
And the Tsar's Men who arrest him
have Basmanov-father at their head.

Through the darkness advances a Royal army.

The outpost at Bitch's Bridgehead.
An exact repetition of the scene.

But the voivode arrested
is Prince Khokholkov-Rostovsky.

And the Tsar's Men are headed
by Fyodor Basmanov.

Through the darkness advances a Royal army.

FADE OUT

FADE IN

THE TSAR'S HALL IN THE
ALEXANDROV LIBERTY

A feast for the dead.
The Tsar and his Tsar's Men in monastic habits.

Above the Tsar and his Tsar's Men,
on a sky background, across a vaulted ceiling,
forty martyrs are painted.
They look down.
Their golden crowns twinkle.

Fedka is chanting in ringing tones.
He stands behind a lectern.
He is amusing himself with Ivan's favorite jest:
he holds a psalter in front of himself upside down.
In ringing tones, a shameless hymn about the executed
he strikes up in a high falsetto:

A chorus repeats after him.

FEDKA:
. . . May they rest with thy saints,
O Christ,
The souls of the boyars and voivodes—
Rebellious—
Who in these days betrayed the outposts of the Tsar,
Accepted gold, silver and fine words . . .
Dully clash one against the other
feasting cups—six pairs:
so that they clang like bells.
. . . for the sake of enriching their wallets . . .
The cups clash. One pair.
And accomplishing Satan's works,
The cups clash. Another pair.

Sold the realm for silver,
The cups clash. A third pair.
  Opened the gates to the Germans . . .
The cups clash. All.
Intones Fyodor:
  . . . And at last have reached a haven . . .
THE CHORUS OF TSAR'S MEN:
  . . . Where shall be no
  Sickness, sorrow,
  Or sighing
  Throughout life eternal . . .
In a ritual dance.
"Making a song out of graveside sobbing . . ."
they have swung to the rapid clangor of mugs.

Have mercy on me, O Lord, have mercy on me . . .

Most ringing of all—the voice of Fedka Basmanov.
He is avoiding the gaze of his father.
He does not want to meet the eyes of the German, Staden.

The elder Basmanov cannot tear his gaze away from his son.

At the center of the board—Tsar Ivan.
Behind the Tsar—is painted the paradisiacal City of Heaven.
But the Tsar looks in front of him.
Concentrated, moody and meditating . . .

The daredevil chant continues.
FEDKA:
  May they rest with thy saints,
  O Christ,
  The souls of the boyars and voivodes—
  Treasonous—
  Who scorch in Hellfire,
  Boil in caldrons like lobsters . . .
Dully clash one upon the other
feasting cups—six pairs:
so that they clang like bells.
  With their heads chopped off,
The cups clash. A pair.
  Made naught upon the block,
The cups clash. Another pair.

Or shamefully hanging by the noose,
The cups clash. A third pair.
     In Moscow like serf carrion . . .
The cups clash. All.
Intones Fyodor:
     . . . *And in coming days shall dwell* . . .
The Chorus of Tsar's Men:
     . . . *Where shall be no*
     Sickness and sorrow,
     Or sighing
     Throughout life eternal . . .
In a ritual dance,
"Making a song out of graveside sobbing . . ."
they have swung to the rapid clangor of mugs.

The more fervent the motif,
the more moody the Tsar.

The more shameless the motif,
the more gloomy the Tsar.

And suddenly the Tsar interrupts the singing:
He says:
The duty of a Tsar's Man—
this duty is no jesting matter.

All have become quiet.
Barely audible in the silence
solitary cups tinkle.
The tinkling has finished.

. . . But there are amongst us even such
whose duty as Tsar's Men
they have bartered for gain . . .

The Tsar's Men press close to one another . . .
The Tsar continues:

There are those here who betray the Tsar's trust.
Their sacred oaths—
as Tsar's Men—
they vend . . .

As the speech continues
the tension grows.
The Tsar's Men sit white-faced:
each is thinking—am I one who is spoken of?

Fyodor looks Staden straight in the eye.
Staden's strength leaves him.
He feverishly gropes for his dagger:
Have mercy on me, HERR GOTT, *have mercy on me—*
he strains through his teeth.

The Tsar continues relentlessly:
There is an eldest amongst you,
to whom the greatest trust was shown . . .
Ivan looks in front of him.

But the Tsar's Men, looking at one another,
gradually begin all
to look in one direction . . .

The Tsar continues:
But this unworthy one has betrayed that trust.
Betrayed the Tsar.
Shamed forever the glorious dignity of a Tsar's Man by his greed . . .

All look in one direction—
at the old Basmanov.

The Basmanov does not see their gaze.
With a look of stone,
staring in his cup, he sits.

The Tsar also has looked at Basmanov.
He has transferred his heavy gaze.

Basmanov the father has jumped up.

Fyodor has looked away into a corner.

Basmanov the father has stared at his son.
He whispers:
Surely not my son? . . .

Fyodor is silent.
He does not look at his father . . .
Basmanov has turned toward the Tsar.
He has wished to justify himself.

And suddenly he sees—
near the elbow of the Tsar a salver.
On the salver grapes.
The Tsar takes a bunch.
He lifts them to his mouth.

But that salver is being proffered by the former bondsman of the Princes
Staritsky,

the former lieutenant of Basmanov,
Demyan Teshata.
Demyan smiles cunningly.

Basmanov relaxes.
He has heaved a sigh:
Not my son . . .
Glory be to God.

And resignedly he gets up from behind the board.

He stands in the middle of the hall.
His head lowered.

For the first time
the son has looked at his father.
His face is wrung with sorrow.

A sorrow that
the father fails to perceive:
he stands with lowered head . . .

The Tsar passes around those present with his eye:
Who is worthy to chop off so wise a head?

All have looked down.
Only Malyuta looks at Ivan.

The glance of Ivan glides sadly
along the faces of the Tsar's Men.

. . . *One wavering in his fearful oath* . . .

The Tsar has halted his glance on Fyodor.
The head of Fyodor Basmanov is lowered . . .

Fyodor has felt on himself the Tsar's gaze.
As though against its will, Fyodor's head lifts.
With open gaze Fyodor looks straight in the eyes of Ivan.

And a great test the Tsar imposes upon Fyodor:
almost imperceptibly he nods to Fyodor . . .

Fyodor Basmanov has got up from behind the board.
He has gone up to his father.
He has led the old man off.

On the way he has looked at Staden.

Staden has understood that his, the German's, life
holds only by one thread, the life of Basmanov the father,
and that for this life of Basmanov the father the end has come . . .
And beneath the glance of Fyodor the German fidgets.

Fyodor has turned away.
He has led away his father.

Led him out.

Demyan smiles in the wake of father and son . . .

The Tsar has spat through his teeth:
And him, the traitor, to the dogs to tear!

THE DARK

In the dark stand the Basmanovs.
Father and son.

They are silent.

The father speaks:

Be not grieved. I was tempted. I sinned.
I fell. . . . The fault is mine. For you a lesson.
Let me embrace you before death!

He embraces his son.

And suddenly, in a passionate whisper,
the father speaks into the ear of his son,
so that none shall have heard.

I have gathered mountains of gold.
All saved for my son.
For the seed of the Basmanovs . . .

The son is moved.
The father continues:

Only for you did I take this sin on my soul.
Break my oath.
Not for myself. For you.
Yearning for you. Having lost you.
Caring for you.
Killing for you.

The son is afraid.
He questions.

But was that not sin?
Not treachery?
Is it not for that you are about to perish at my hand?

The father speaks passionately:
Death does not frighten me. . . . That my seed may live.
Enrich and multiply.
That sons—grandsons—great-grandsons may grow,
that in those sons—grandsons—great-grandsons
I may forever live.
For that Basmanov faces his execution firm,
that my sons—grandsons—great-grandsons
with the Tsar's sons—grandsons—great-grandsons
may vie in ages yet to come.

So that with my gold I with Ivan
after my death may vie:
who knows who shall prevail?
who knows whose seed is more fit to live?
And which tree in the course of ages shall outgrow another? . . .

Fyodor hears these words treasonable,
tempting.

He hearkens.

With hungry gaze—
his last, fore-death—

the father, sorrow-laden,
into the son's eyes looks.

He hears the summons of his blood
in his son's blood.
But he also sees wavering.
It is as though the fearful oath
echoes in the air,
holds back Fyodor from decision . . .

And the father grasps the son's fair neck
in his mighty—
Basmanov—
hands.
I'll choke you . . . —he croaks.
Swear before my death
that you'll not be bound
by the fearful oath!

The hands of Fyodor grope on the breast of his father.
His eyes look afar off, into the years.

His oath as Tsar's Man, which he is about to betray,
he soundlessly repeats, with paling lips:
. . . *To renounce kith and kin,*
forget sire and dear mother . . .

His fingers toward the cross next his father's skin,
under the tunic,
reach out . . .

Swear, that you'll hide all from Ivan's line!
Swear, that you'll hide all for the Basmanov line!

It has grown dark before the eyes of Fyodor:
he is strangling in his father's grip.
He has blurted hoarsely:
I swear!
And has touched his lips to the cross next his father's breast.

And with that superhuman kiss,
the Basmanovs have bidden each other farewell forever . . .

You have lifted my burden . . . the father has heaved a sigh.
The son has straightened himself: *The Tsar waits—'tis time to finish.*

Says the father:
I shall pray . . . *While I yet pray, finish me* . . .
even as, together, we finished the traitor Turuntay-Pronsky.
With that same blow that I myself taught you at Kazan.

He has turned away into a corner.
Undone his collar.
Bent his head,
stretched out his neck.
Whispered a prayer . . .

In the darkness has flashed the sword of Fyodor Basmanov
and clean taken off the gray head of Basmanov-father.

THE HALL

A closed door . . .

Anxiously at the closed door,
looks Tsar's-Man Staden.

A knife blade trembles in the hand of the German Tsar's Man . . .

Yet more anxiously
Tsar Ivan watches the door:
he is in anguish . . .

The door has been flung open.
Fyodor has appeared.

His head is lowered.
His hair is stuck to his forehead.

He has raised his head.

He looks Ivan straight in the eye.

But Fedka's gaze has already become deceitful:
it turns away.

The Tsar's lips have twitched.

He has pronounced thickly:
You did not spare your own father, Fyodor.
How then will you bring yourself to spare and protect me? . . .

The young Basmanov has understood—
Ivan has divined his secret pact with his father . . .

He has wanted to speak:
too late.

The curt order has rung out:
ARREST HIM!

Like one crazed, Fedka tries to fling himself at the Tsar.

The path to the latter
in a bound .
Staden has barred.

He plunges his knife into Fyodor.

The hunched figure of Ivan slumps on his throne:
So—now the Basmanovs have ceased to be . . .

Fyodor lies motionless.
With a glassy stare, upwards
at the crowns of the forty martyrs
looks the dying man.

A solitary tear
down the gray beard
of Tsar Ivan rolls . . .
At the end of the beard it hangs,
as though made out of graveside sobbing.
Have mercy on me, O God, have mercy on me . . .

Someone's cup has tinkled quietly.
Become silent . . .

Suddenly in panic the eyes
of the dying man light up;
with an effort Fyodor raises himself on his elbow.

With his last strength
from death's embrace
he pulls himself back.

His last duty—
on the grave's edge—
he fulfills:
. . . *The German, Tsar, trust him not!* . . . —
he shouts to the Tsar.

His curly hair
has fallen back.

He is dead . . .

Like a fallen angel,
Fyodor lies on the floor.
With his black habit,
like wings,
sprawled over the flagstones . . .

The Tsar raises his heavy eyelids—
his gaze comes to a rest on the German Staden.
With an ill lightness does the foreign guest
on the Tsar's behalf
against the Tsar's own liege man
intervene . . .

On Staden's shoulder
the heavy hand of Malyuta
descends.

His teeth chattering,

Staden, from under Malyuta's hand,
strives to extricate himself:

the hand is heavy—he remains held.

Suddenly there is a pealing of bells outside.
All have turned round.
And into the chamber precipitately bursts a messenger:
THE LIVONIANS ARE COMING!

All else is forgotten.

All have jumped up from their places.
Ivan's eyes have blazed.
With savage joy he utters through his teeth:
Thou hast fallen into the trap, Prince Andrew!

Malyuta has exclaimed:
You've fallen into it, Kurbsky . . .

Ivan has shouted at the top of his voice:
ON THE MARCH!

Black cloaks have been thrown aside.
Tunics have gleamed gold.
Blades have flashed from their sheaths.

To Livonia!—
is the cry.

And Malyuta cries:
TO THE BALTIC!
And see, already, the light playing upon them,
the horsemen of Rus are whirling to the border.

Together with the horsemen whirls a song:
> *Ocean-sea,*
> *Azure sea,*
> *Azure sea,*
> *Glorious sea* . . .
The Tsar's banners sparkle.
Their golden suns blazing.

Gallop the Tsar's Men
and gold blaze their tunics.
> *Arises today*
> *To defend Muscovy.*
> *A terrible host,*
> *It goes to the sea*
> *To beat off the foe*
> *For our loved country* . . .
Sharply beat the little tabors,
borne beneath the saddles of all the riders.
And this drum roll urges on their war-horses . . .
> *The ocean-sea*
> *To win with the spear,*
> *So that ships may pass*
> *On every side* . . .
Gallops Tsar Ivan.

Gallops Malyuta;
the regiments follow him.
Their armor sits tight on them,
and they seem as though cast out of lead.
> *Ocean-sea,*
> *Azure sea,*
> *Azure sea,*
> *Russian sea!*

KURBSKY'S TENT

Night. Great luxury.
Lighted candelabras.
Much silver plate.

And yet greater disorder:
higgledy-piggledy—cannonballs, cases of gunpowder,
rich weapons and luxurious armor.

Scattered on a low table
military maps.

And near them,
as though with the rational game of strategy
were mingled crazy games of hazard,
are strewn gaming cards
and gambling dice:
more fit indeed for such a crazy venture
as this campaign against Moscow.

To Kurbsky runs in the envoy-German
who was present at that audience with Elizabeth of England.
And the madness of the march on Moscow becomes obvious.

The Muscovite has caught us in a trap;
Ginger Bess is on his side!

Kurbsky furious:
The ginger witch has cheated us.

We must retreat at once!—cries Kurbsky.
We must attack!—cries the German.
Like lightning we must dash for Moscow—
the way is clear,
the outposts bought!

Thanks be to the Almighty!—
Kurbsky pathetically bends the knee.

Raising his arms aloft, he exclaims:
My beloved country!
Receive and embrace thy loving son!
A horde of foes
he dispatches forthwith upon his fatherland.

T o M o s c o w ! —
the traitor cries.

The trumpeters bring their trumpets to their lips.
They have not time to start the fanfares:
in the silence suddenly
a deep discharge resounds—
a cannon . . .

And after it—a second.
A third.

Kurbsky is at a loss.

The trumpeters have lowered their trumpets.

Heavy gunfire afar off.

Flies in a runner:
The outpost at Rotten Marsh encountered us with fire!

Thou liest!—in anger cries Kurbsky.

Rushes in a second runner:
The outpost at Crooked Stream—they met us with fire!

Yet more angrily cries Kurbsky:
A lie!

Comes tottering in a third runner:
At Bitch's Bridgehead—in uncountable number,
Russian troops!

The German has rushed out of the tent.

Suffocating with rage,
unable to find words,
foaming at the mouth,
Kurbsky throws himself on the fallen runner.
Lifts him,
shakes him in fury.

From a hillock, into the camp,
the Russians are firing
incendiary projectiles.

Brothers Foma and Yeroma Chokhov
are the officers in command.

Handsome—bearded,
in voivode dress.

We recognize among the new
and old guns:
"Nightingale."
"Lion "
"Bully Boy."

Handsome, bearded,
the brothers Chokhov:
Foma and Yeroma.

And, as formerly,
with youthful mischief,
as one time at Kazan,
their eyes sparkle.

Just as in bygone days
they bandy jests:

FOMA:
We're old men, you and I . . .
YEROMA:
But our guns are hearty!

FOMA:
Foma makes "Nightingale" sing true . . .
YEROMA:
And Yeroma makes "Bully Boy" gambol . . .

The gunners laugh.
The guns thunder a salvo.

Kurbsky, raging, thrusts aside the runner.
The runner falls amid a pile of silver dishes.
Suddenly a cannonball carries away the top of the tent.

The camp is seen to be afire.
Kurbsky only just manages
to escape from his tent.

Into the tent flies an incendiary projectile.

At full gallop in flies Malyuta.
By his side Peter Volynets.
The tent is empty.
The projectile sizzles.

Malyuta's steed tramples its broad hoofs on the debris:
on the playing cards and on the fighting charts.
And it is plain from both the one and the other
that the game is lost.

The tent is empty:
a luxurious suit of armor glitters in a corner.

Volynets has raised its visor with the end of his six-edged mace:
inside is empty.
Skipped!
He has drawn back his mace . . .

The gilded armor has swayed,
crashed down.
With the sound of an empty bucket
it has rolled to the feet of Malyuta . . .

Don't dawdle, Volynets!
Malyuta has reared up his horse.
After him, quick!

The tent has burst into flames.

Into a black column of smoke ascending to the sky,
it has exploded.
Malyuta has rushed away.
Volynets barely keeps up with him.

Against the background of a rosy glow whirls along with the horsemen—
Tsar Ivan.
Hair streaming in the wind.
Nostrils dilated.
His eyes burn:
Now shall we, like our forbear,
the great ruler Alexander Nevsky,
drive without mercy the Germans from our soil! . . .

The Tsar seems rejuvenated by twenty years.

Against the background of the glow whirls along Tsar Ivan with his
horsemen.

THE CASTLE OF WOLMAR

Night. Darkness. Firing.
Servitors run by with torches.

They cry:
The Russians are coming!!

They leap across a wide bed:
they are saving their skins.

On the bed Kurbsky wakes.
Springs up in horror.

He flees half-clad.

The road to Wolmar.
Whirl by the Russian horsemen.

Wolmar Castle
Tsar Ivan enters.
By his side, Peter Volynets,
Malyuta.
Ivan exclaims joyfully:
These German cities do not await the trial of battle,
but of themselves bow their proud heads!

Still more delightedly Ivan cries out to a scribe
the end of the text of another epistle to Kurbsky:
. . . And where didst thou think, Kurbsky, to rest
from thy labors—
in Wolmar?
Even thither has God brought us upon thy head!
And even thence have we, with God's help, driven thee forth!

Into the room burst Latvian peasants;
they drag behind them struggling,
disheveled, the German Tsar's Man
Henryk Staden.

They fling themselves on their knees before Ivan.
Ivan asks:
What is this?

The peasants speak:
He has pillaged our property,
set our village afire!

Staden seeks to justify himself.

Ivan assails him angrily:
We have not come here as conquerors,
but back to our primordial land!
He has turned to the peasants:
Who are these?

Villeins of the Livonian Order—they answer.
They hold out callused hands to the Tsar.

And Ivan bids:
Distribute grain!
Let them till our own
—ours now and forever—
Russian soil!

The peasants have rushed to Ivan, surrounded him.

This is too much for Staden.

And, giving vent to a curse, he leaps out through the window.
The peasants hurl themselves after him.
The sound of flails lingers on the air . . .

And Ivan dictates to his scrivener-clerk
the finish of the letter to Kurbsky:

Written upon our native Livonian soil,
in the city
of Wolmar
in the year 7086 (15//).

The road to Weissenstein.
Cannon on the move.
In front, Foma and Yeroma.

Malyuta gallops by.
The Russian horses gallop by.

The guns roll out onto a hillock.
The guns stand.
"Wolf."
"Lion."
"Basilisk."

Foma and Yeroma are exchanging banter.
Handsome,
bearded,
clad in voivode dress.

FOMA:
Watch how Foma makes the Lion roar!
YEROMA:
And Yeroma—the Basilisk sting!

Boom!—
has thundered "Basilisk"
with all its muzzle,
saving Yeroma the trouble.

WEISSENSTEIN CASTLE.
SUNRISE

A great Gothic hall.
Guns thunder in the distance.

The cannonade is coming nearer.

Feverishly the huge chandeliers quiver.
One is made out of antlers,
with a gilt madonna in the middle.

At the table is the Vogt of Weissenstein,
Kaspar von Oldenbock.
(Sometime—long ago—he came with an embassy
to the young Ivan,
and spectators will remember him from the prologue of the film.)

Now the aged Vogt
is deathly pale.

Around Oldenbock—
knights.
A chaplain.
Gentlemen-at-arms.
Worried ladies.

On one side—Prince Kurbsky.

Says von Oldenbock:
To fight this barbarian
is impossible . . .
He leads Tartar as well as Russian hordes.

Our own slaves—
Ests, Lats, Lits—
fight on his side.

At Wolmar he distributed to them draft cattle.
At Wenden he gave out grain.

From border to border they await the Muscovy barbarian.
And recognize him as their lawful Tsar . . .

Having lowered his voice, he has added:
Our very garrison
went over to the side of the Russians in the night!

Death to the turncoats!—
Kurbsky cries piercingly.

A general movement.
All rise from their places.

Paler than Oldenbock,
Kurbsky cries:
Flee, flee!
The earth holds none stronger than the Russian warrior!

A cold voice remarks scathingly:
To the Turncoat Prince
this is well known . . .
from his glorious battle near Nevel! *

And we see, also at the table, the fat,
unsuccessful German emissary to Elizabeth . . .

Kurbsky has leaped up in fury.
He wants to throw himself on the offender . . .

The deafening thunder
of a cannonade close by.
Kurbsky recognizes the gun's voice:
That's "Nightingale"!

Another roar.
Kurbsky cries:
"Lion"!
"Wolf"!
"Singer"!
"Bully Boy"!
Ivan's favorite cannon!
Utterly horrified, he screams:
That means the Terrible himself is near!

A thunderous shot:
"Basilisk"! . . .

* See p. 119.

And nobody knows
whether to the gun
or to the Tsar
that horror-struck cry referred.

General confusion.
Someone falls on his knees.

From their knees appeal
to Christ and to the Madonna
ladies in prayer.

Kurbsky cries hysterically:
Flee, lest it be too late!

Says von Oldenbock:
Honor does not permit us to save ourselves by flight . . .
He has explained to the German emissary:
If we did, our slaves of yesterday
would string us up . . .

The Vogt goes to a small secret door.
He opens it.
Whosoever lacks honor may flee . . .

A pause.
All look at Kurbsky.
Loud sounds the cannonade.

Kurbsky tears himself from his place.
Rushes to the opening.
We hear the tinkle of departing spurs . . .

But we . . .

To the Vogt they bring a golden chain.
They put it on him.
The chain weighs twenty-one pounds.

We . . .

The Vogt has given a sign to the musicians' gallery.

With a deafening din the orchestra has started up.

The growing cannonade
it strives to drown.

From a little wicket darts out
Kurbsky.
A servitor holds a horse.
KURBSKY.
One horse? What about you?

THE SERVITOR:
The Vogt, sir, knew
that only one horse would be needed . . .

Kurbsky has slashed the servitor with a whip.
Has galloped off through the shrubbery.

The servitor goes back to the wicket.
Presses on a lever.
Stones block the exit behind Kurbsky.

Reckless with the knowledge that they have no way out,
the knights and gentlemen-at-arms
have dashed to the ladies.

Flows beer.
Whirls the dance.
The sound of the cannonade and of a battering ram's blows.

The orchestra plays.
The hall shakes.

All have stopped. All are listening.
In the pause: the dull pounding of the rams.

Pound the rams.
Pound the guns.

Hysterically whirls the dance.

Pound the guns.

Pound the rams.

With the German jester-diplomat
to another secret door
Oldenbock
goes.

He says:
But we . . .
go to invoke the Almighty . . .

With the German diplomat
by a stone staircase
he descends to a vault.

The vault they enter is an underground chapel.

The pounding of the rams rumbles in the distance.
The dancing in the hall above sounds dully.

Pounding.

Dancing.

Pounding.

Dancing.

The Russian trumpets blow—calling to the assault.

Ivan dispatches three captains
to lead his armies.

Malyuta gnaws his fingernails in rage.
He is green with envy.

The trumpets blow.
The Russians have given the word of command . . .

All is dully audible in the vault:
with a far-off clash
the Russians have surged into the assault . . .

Oldenbock applies his torch to a fuse.

The assault surges

Dancing.
Prancing.

Explosion!
A wall has collapsed.

The dance has stopped.

Von Oldenbock rejoices.
The jester trembles.

The dance goes on, more frantic than before.

The trumpets have sounded.
A trampling is heard.
The dance continues.

The rams ram.
Two Russians, known to us from the Siege of Kazan,
are steadily working at the rams.
They hear the beat of the dance music.
One says to the other:
Ugh, and wouldn't Tsar Ivan have given it to us hot
if we'd thus defended a castle!

Trampling is heard.
Oldenbock applies the torch to a second fuse.

The troops are scrambling to the attack.

The dance goes on.
The rams pound.

Oldenbock listens tensely.

Explosion!

The hall crumbles in.

The troops have recoiled.
The troops run back.

Von Oldenbock rejoices.
He flings himself on his knees before the altar.

The troops run back.

They come running to Ivan.
Ivan in a fury:
Forward!—he roars;
raging, from Peter Volynets
he tears the Tsar's standard.
Plunges among the troops.

Malyuta rises up in his path.
He towers before Ivan like a stone wall.
He will not let Ivan pass:
Your job is to build the State.
Not to crawl amidst gunpowder!

He falls to his knees:
I'll go.
Twenty years I have waited for this honor.
Give me the standard!

Ivan looks around:
the troops have huddled in flocks—
they are afraid of the explosions.
He has to decide . . .

He hands the standard to Malyuta.
Thou only art left to me . . .
The last!
The sole.
He kisses him on the forehead.

He makes the sign of the cross on Malyuta's forehead.
He sends him to the bastion.

274

Winged by the Tsar's embrace,
Malyuta has let out a roar.

The trumpets have taken up that roar.
The Tsar's standard has flown aloft.
The troops have dashed into the attack.

Oldenbock has given a start.
He does not believe his ears:
The Russian troops are flinging themselves into the attack again?

He has dragged the covering off the altar:
the altar is constructed of boxes of gunpowder.
Like a black snake a fuse coils itself along the ground.

Malyuta runs up to the walls.
From bastion to bastion he clambers.
Not clambers—soars.
Volynets cannot keep up with Malyuta.

The trumpets blare.
The troops clamber to the attack.

Oldenbock lights the last—third—fuse . . .
The fuse has caught light.

Malyuta soars from bastion to bastion.
He leads the troops behind him.

In the vault, suddenly,
a howl of despair.
The German has realized,
he has flung himself at Oldenbock in terror of death,
he strives to reach the fuse, he wants to extinguish it.
Oldenbock holds the German in an iron grasp.
He does not let him reach the fuse.

The fire runs along the fuse.

Malyuta climbs the wall.

Ivan in ecstasy watches his favorite.

Volynets can't keep up with Malyuta.
He hurries. He stumbles.
He drops behind Malyuta.
He falls.

With a howl the German has broken away.
He has thrust back Oldenbock..
Seized the fuse in his teeth.

He has torn out the fuse . . .
He rolls on the ground with the fuse.
Extinguishes it with his body.

Malyuta has flown aloft onto the wall;
he has cried:
Prince Andrew, do you hear me!

Somewhere through marshes Kurbsky gallops.
A shot.
He has hurtled from his horse.
He has fled through the marsh like a hare.

Malyuta has raised high the standard.

Oldenbock has grabbed the torch.
He has swung the torch.
The German has seen,
with a cry thrown himself at Oldenbock.

Malyuta plants the standard
in triumph upon the wall.

The German is choking Oldenbock.
Over the German, Oldenbock
flings the torch into the boxes of gunpowder.

A third explosion—the last—resounds.

The turret above gives a leap.

Stones and beams crash down in destruction on Malyuta.

The Tsar's standard is indestructible; it seethes like gold in the dust.

Ivan issues commands in a frenzy.
He hurries with troops to help Malyuta.

With superhuman strength, an arch
Malyuta holds off himself with one hand,
his free hand stretching aloft the standard.
He shouts for a relief.

The Tsar and his troops hasten.

The debris crumbles heavily on Malyuta.

Malyuta is holding a wall up with one hand;
with the other he holds aloft the standard.
With a deep groan he cries for a relief.

The troops fly to the attack.
Over the fragments of the turret, Peter Volynets
scrambles to Malyuta.

The wall is crumpling . . .
Subsides.
Malyuta is holding the wall up with one hand.
His knees and legs are set to resist it.
He passes the standard to Volynets.

Peter takes the standard.
He wants to help Malyuta.

Malyuta roars at him:
Don't dawdle, Volynets!

The wall is crumpling.

Both you and the standard will perish!
He has overtaxed his strength:
Get up higher: thrust that standard into the very sky!

The wall crumples with a rumble.

It settles down on Malyuta.

Malyuta's bones crack.
The veins of his bullneck swell.
His eyes bulge from their sockets.
The blood flows from under his fingernails.
He roars in frenzy:
Get away! Dog's devil!!!
He is hoarse:
Love Ivan—there's no one to care for him! . . .

Tears have gushed from the eyes of Volynets.
He has flung aloft the standard.

It has soared up over the ruins of the turret;
the standard blazes against the sky like a star.
Malyuta has beheld it and
then, as though
with the wall and the beams,
come tumbling down.

Volynets has planted the standard.

Malyuta has rolled to the bottom . . .
Ivan has rushed up to Malyuta.
Bent over Malyuta.
Around them rages the assault.

Malyuta has gazed:
the standard flies above on the walls of the castle;
it blazes, a second sun in the sky.

Malyuta whispers:
I'm sorry for one thing . . . not to see the sea . . .

Ivan has risen to his height:
Thou shalt see it!

Malyuta is lifted onto a stretcher.

The woods are afire.
The Russians are advancing.

The Livonian knights are fleeing.

Headlong
Kurbsky is fleeing across the marshes . . .
He has sunk in the mire . . .

On a knoll, Ivan and Malyuta.
Smell it?
The nostrils of both are dilated.
The wind's salt.

And once more the pursuit.
Russians smiting Livonians.

And once more the knoll.
On the knoll, Ivan and Malyuta.
Hear it?
And through the music of battle
comes the distant steady beating of the waves.
I hear it . . .

At the feet of Ivan fall banners.

Thunder the cannon.

By a cannon, Foma.

Gallop the horsemen;
in the van, Yeroma.

And through the chaos of hoofbeats,
firing and trumpets,
steadily comes the beating of the waves
and the roar of the now not distant sea . . .

And see, Ivan and Malyuta are now upon a dune.
Malyuta's strength has ebbed.
Around, all is as though hushed.
Malyuta's eyes are closed.

And softly Ivan whispers to him:
See it?

Afar off is a narrow strip
of the Baltic Sea.
Over the sea run whitecaps.

Malyuta has raised himself a little.
His eyes are wide open.
He shouts in a ringing voice:
I see it!

And he is dead.

And the billows have roared out in answer to Malyuta.
Once again they are swelling and crashing.
And the trumpets blare.

And, spellbound, forward to the waves
goes Tsar Ivan,
And the sea does him homage.

And the waves bow slowly to his feet.
And they lick the feet
of the Autocrat of All Rus.

And henceforward even to eternity
shall the seas continue obedient to the Russian State . . .

The Tsar has turned back to his troops.

Peter looks at him.
Foma looks.
Yeroma looks.
The old look at him.
The young look at him.
The Russian host looks at him.

And in answer to the words of the Tsar the troops have roared.
The trumpets have rejoiced.
The sea has thundered.
The billows have surged.
  ON THE SEAS WE STAND
  AND SHALL STAND!
There comes from the screen
the finish of the film:
  Ocean-sea!
  Azure sea,
  Azure sea,
  Russian sea!

THE END

NOTES ON THE TRANSLATION

THE LAYOUT

Since a great part of the interest of the scenario lies in the line arrangement of Eisenstein's original, this has, with the rarest of exceptions, been exactly preserved in translation. Of course, a line-for-line translation of poetry is impossible, but here the task was comparatively simple. No scansion was required; it was necessary only to preserve euphony and as much as possible of Eisenstein's laconism, and to hint here and there at his play on words, while regarding ease of reading and ready comprehension as having paramount priority.

Included in the chopped prose of the screenplay are some actual songs, lyrics written not by Eisenstein but by a colleague, Vladimir Lugovsky. My co-translator, Herbert

Marshall, worked with Lugovsky for a time on an English version of the lyrics adjusted to the musical score. But since the main consideration here has been their subtle relation to the drama, we have preferred to stick close to their literal meaning rather than attempt musicality.

THE ARCHAISM

The original Russian is constantly, deliberately, antiquated. An attempt has been made to fit the wording to the stylistic pastiche of the dramatic texture. In a film, where cinematic directions ("fade in," "pan," "off screen") occur, however occasionally, the attempt is a dangerous one. At every moment one risks falling through thin ice and producing a "Ye Olde Tudor Close-uppe" effect, so to speak.

Eisenstein's text revels in archaic Russian vocables and forms. There is no option but to follow as far as taste will allow.

"THEE" AND "THOU"

"Thee" and "Thou" constitute in English a special problem, absent from the original. Modern Russian —like modern French and modern German—distinguishes the second-person singular from the second-person plural, as English has ceased to do. Shall a film scenario adopt the stiff old forms and bury the humanity of common speech or shall it risk a modern, slang effect that might disrupt the ancient pomp and circumstance of formal address? We have compromised. Thus clerics always and Ivan, except in moments of greatest intimacy and informality, use the singular. So do courtiers. Groundlings and those Ivan raised "from the dung" use the colloquial "you." However illogical this may be, it "feels" right. For the plural sense, we have eschewed "ye" throughout.

RUSSICISMS

Literal translation from the Russian always risks retaining so many alien words—or so many footnotes— as to bewilder the reader and remove all possibility of his settling amid the drama with an ease equal to that of the Russian reader of the original. On the other hand, a few exotic words, the more familiar the better, are acceptable to preserve authenticity.

Where the archaic flavor is as essential as the geographic and cultural, if the reader is to be transported effectively to Ivan's world, special trouble has been taken to reduce the alien elements and emphasize the period ones.

Thus, for proper names, only those of commoners and—among the courtiers—those without easy English (Greek or Latin derivative) equivalents have been retained in their original Russian form. "Andrew," "Eustace," "Euphrosyne," and "Peter" interfere far less with apprehension of the drama as a Renaissance contest than would "Andrei," "Yestafy," "Yefrosinia," and "Pyotr." We have dispensed with patronymics and feminine endings altogether.

Likewise with geographical names —"Headfall Ring" for "Lobnoye Mesto" (literally, "Foreheady Place") is obvious, considering its significance. The "Sloboda" ("Alexandrov Sloboda") to which Ivan retired to lead a far from monastic existence with his "iron brotherhood" is usually translated "suburb." That is what the word has come to mean, in modern Russian, for the "Slobodas" were outside the city; with their own expansion, and that of the city to which they formed a periphery, that is what they became. But of course this word, in meaning as well as sound, would be a hopeless anachronism. The perfectly good medieval equivalent is "Liberty," meaning a place where a person or persons not subject to the same laws as the region outside its limits had received leave and license to own or settle. Thus the Abbey at St. Albans had a "Liberty" at Abbots Langley. Ivan's Moscow had a "German" Liberty, assigned to foreigners; his palace at the Alexandrov Liberty was about a hundred miles from Moscow.

Almost the only Russian words retained are those everyone knows—"Tsar" (Emperor), "boyar" (nobleman), "icon" (sacred image), "ruble" (a coin). "Voivode" (military officer at this time; later, after border regions had been long under military government, it sometimes meant "governor"), and "sarafan" (the long-skirted Russian national dress worn not only by peasants but also sometimes, even in the nineteenth century, by court ladies at special balls) may be less familiar. "Kokoshnik"—the coronet that goes with the "sarafan"—we have replaced with "tiara." "Tunic" for "khalat" is less happy, for a khalat is certainly longer than a tunic, though likewise belted round; but it occurs so frequently, and in dramatic contexts, that the Russian word just had to go. Likewise there could be no question of retaining "oprichnik," and little of "strelets"—which would throw into the mind of the reader at each tense moment a confusing reminder of what he knew or didn't know about Russian history.

Most English feudal terms have such a Latin flavor that one scruples to employ them. Thus "villeins" appears odd for "obrochniki," but what else can they be called? People who pay quit-rent are not exactly serfs. German medievalism comes to the rescue with "Vogt," which in the West would probably be a "Bailiff" or a "Seneschal."

The Slavonic church, being Byzantine, takes its Bible from the Greek, and even Biblical names therefore differ from those familiar to the Englishman, whose Bible comes from Hebrew. We have retained "Sabaoth" in place of "Jehovah," for this Greek word is at least known and has an exotic grandeur that is extraordinarily apt, but we boggled at calling Shadrach, Meshach, and Abednego by what are apparently their Greek testament names—Ananiya, Azariya, and Misail—so here is one more inconsistency that only taste can answer for.

"Fyodor" and "Fedka"

Readers will notice how often we use a diminutive—"Fedka" for "Fyodor" (Eisenstein used several, as the Russian language can, e.g., "Fedya"), in the case of the young Basmanov. The father naturally uses the "straight" name for his son only in moments of solemn formality between them. Intimacy between father and son, as well as between Tsar and protégé, demands the informality of the pet name. Eisenstein was not concerned to emphasize the bisexuality recounted of Ivan by his enemies and traditional in Russian story, but it would have been impossible for him to render authentically the relationship between Ivan and young Basmanov—spasmodic condescension in the former, constant presumption in the latter—while always using "Fyodor." So in this we have carefully followed the author's own subtle differentiation.

The "Terrible"

One more point—Ivan's own name. Some bright Russian translators, having come to the conclusion from their knowledge of current English that "Grozny" is not "Terrible," have recently been suggesting, and even employing, a frightful locution—"Ivan the Dread."

Of course Ivan was not "terrible" in the sense in which that word is most employed nowadays—"What a terrible party (or movie or traffic jam)." Ivan himself had no doubt what he meant by "Grozny." He wrote at length about it and said he had to be "Grozny." He meant that to be "Royal," to command respect as someone towering above all other temporal powers and of a different quality from them, he must inspire fear, reverence, awe. Indeed, there is no doubt that (God forbid it should be used) the most exact translation of "Ivan Grozny" is "Ivan the Awful." Unfortunately this word also has acquired an unsuitable modern overlay. But "Terrible" still retains enough of its original flavor, and in the form "John the Terrible" it was good enough for Queen Elizabeth I and Sir John Chancellor. So let it suffice for this book.

I. M.

NOTES ON THE FILM TRANSCRIPTS

By Soviet regulation, a "Montazhny List" (or Transcript) of each film issued must be prepared and registered. This transcript narrates in sequence the content of each shot, its length, and the accompanying sound.

It is the third stage of documentation for every studio production. First comes the scenario, the author's account of his visualization of the film as it should appear on the screen. That, for *Ivan*, comprises the main body of this book. Then the shooting script, together with the various specialized sets of instructions issued for translating the scenario into celluloid. These include the sketches furnished to art directors in charge of sets, make-up, and the preparation of period properties. In the case of *Ivan*, over

2,000 such drawings were made, and most of them survive. With Eisenstein, the process of drawing overlapped the first and subsequent stages. Thus, as he himself tells us in "My Drawings" (*see* page 301), sometimes the drawing of a scene would occur to him before its description in words, sometimes the reverse. And the drawing process would also continue even onto the floor, helping the actor to visualize the task assigned to him and being recast as the work proceeded.

When the film is edited and finished, the transcript records it in its final form. However carefully a film is prepared, unforeseen developments—both negative, in the sense that an idea is frustrated and has to be abandoned, and positive, in that an idea is improved upon in realization—always alters the original conception. What can be done in reality is never identical with that which was hoped for and sought.

The study of a transcript, only less than repeated viewing of a film itself, can therefore reveal comparisons with the scenario of great value to students of technique. But, since this book is not primarily for the specialist, it will suffice here to quote only the Credit and Introductory Titles, followed by a brief reel-by-reel summary (based on the transcripts) that will give the general reader an idea of the principal changes undergone by the films on their way to the screen.

In the transcripts, the length of Part One is given as 827 scenes (counting each title as a numbered scene) and 9,006 feet—that is, about one hour and three quarters projection time. The length of Part Two is given as 744 scenes and 7,821 feet—about an hour and a half.

PART ONE

MAIN AND CREDIT TITLES

1. IVAN THE TERRIBLE
2. *Author of the Scenario and Producer-Director*—Sergei M. Eisenstein
3. *Photography*—Andrei Moskvin (*Interiors*)
   Eduard Tisse (*Exteriors*)
4. *Music*—Sergei Prokofiev
   Lyrics—Vladimir Lugovsky
5. IVAN THE TERRIBLE—Nikolai Cherkasov
6. ANASTASIA ROMANOVNA, *the Tsarina*—Ludmila Tselikovskaya
   EUPHROSYNE STARITSKY, *the Tsar's aunt*—Serafima Birman
   VLADIMIR STARITSKY, *her son*—Pavel Kadochnikov
7. OPRICHNIKS:
   MALYUTA SKURATOV—Mikhail Zharov
   ALEXEY BASMANOV—Amvrosy Buchma
   FYODOR BASMANOV, *his son*—Mikhail Kuznetsov
8. PRINCE ANDREW KURBSKY—Mikhail Nazvanov
   BOYAR FYODOR KOLYCHEV, *subsequently* ABBOT PHILIP—
   Andrei Abrikosov
9. PIMEN, ARCHBISHOP OF NOVGOROD—Alexander Mgebrov
   AN ARCHDEACON—Maxim Mikhailov
   NIKOLA "BIG-FOOL," *a beggar simpleton*—Vsevolod Pudovkin
10. *Associate Director*—V. Sveshnikov
    Assistant Director—L. Indenbom
11. *Art Director for Sets*—Yosip Spinel
    Art Director for Costumes—L. Naumova
    Art Director for Makeup—V. Goryunov
12. *Sound Recordists*—V. Bogdankevitch
    V. Volsky

Conductor—A. Stasyevich
13. *Second Cameraman*—V. Dombrovsky
    Junior Assistant Directors—V. Kuznetsova
                                I. Bir
                                B. Bunayev
14. *Editing Assistant*—E. Tobak
    Floor Secretary—L. Chedin
Available credits not included in the main titles:
    Assistant to Costume Art Director—N. Buzina
    Supervisors of Costume Making—Y. Raizman and M. Safonova
    Supervisor of Set Building—Y. Shakhporonov
    Props—V. Lomov
    Consultant on the Religious Ceremony of the Coronation—
                                Archpriest P. Tsvetkov
    Ambassador of the Livonian Order—S. Timoshenko
    Foreigner—A. Rumnev
    Production—Alma-Ata Film Studio, 1943/4

INTRODUCTORY TITLES

FADE IN
15. This film is about the Man,
16. who, in the XVIth Century first united our country,
17. about the Prince of Muscovy,
18. who out of separate, discordant and autonomous
    principalities created a unified, mighty State,
19. about the Captain, who spread the military
    glory of our motherland to east and west,
20. about the Ruler, who, to achieve these
    great tasks, first took upon himself
21. the crown of Tsar of all Rus.

ACTION ANALYSIS

The most important dramaturgic differences between the finished Part One and the scenario are the omission of the Prologue, the new Introductory Title, the improvement of the scene between Anastasia and Kurbsky at the bedside of the sick Ivan, and the reduction of the Tsar's Men (oprichniks) at the end. In the main the original is followed with amazing fidelity, both in outline and in detail, and the cuts are obviously trims for length or, toward the end, trims of scenes that link with the Second Part, which—if included in Part One, as originally planned—would incline to hang in the air.

Reel One

(All page numbers refer to the scenario as it appears in this book.)
Begins with the Main Title,

Credit Titles, and Introductory Title.

The Prologue in the scenario is omitted.

The action begins with the coronation and at first almost exactly follows the scenario scene as described beginning page 41, except that the first shot shows the Cap of Monomakh, the second the regalia —orb and scepter—and then we proceed to the ceremony and voice of the Metropolitan off screen (page 42), the ambassadors appearing only later.

The ceremony then proceeds according to scenario until completion of the baptism of gold (page 47) and the young Tsar advancing toward the camera.

REEL TWO

Begins with the speech of the newly crowned Ivan (page 50) and follows the scenario version of the rest of the coronation closely up to the remark of the Livonian Ambassador, *He mustn't be strong . . .* (page 58), which in the film is followed, instead of being preceded, by Euphrosyne's muttered threat, *We'll celebrate this "Master's" wedding!* (earlier, same page).

This, in the film, ends the coronation. Then the agitation scene at Headfall Ring is omitted, and a brief scene in which the Livonian Ambassador arouses envy in Prince Kurbsky is all that intervenes before we reach the nuptial feast and a general view of the reveling before the kiss (page 62).

The feast proceeds as in the scenario and the reel ends with the finish of the conversation with Kolychev (page 64).

REEL THREE

Goes straight on, with the servant approaching Euphrosyne (page 65). We hear what he tells her, namely, that a mob is burning the mansions of the Glinskys and Zakharins and is on its way to the palace to make demands of Ivan.

The banquet scene then proceeds, closely following the scenario, right to the end, including the incursion of the people, the emissaries from Kazan, and the final dispersal accompanied by cries of *To Kazan!* (page 77). The only substantial change is that Nikola the Simpleton, his scene at Headfall Ring having been omitted, enters with the crowd and participates in the dialogue.

REEL FOUR

The brief views of the forging of the cannon are omitted, and this reel opens with the cannon being dragged along the roads (page 79).

The siege of Kazan continues much as in scenario, to end of reel, following Ivan's remark to Basmanov-father, *The name of a boyar-hater shall not slip my memory . . .* (page 84).

The only notable difference is that, at the outset, there are several shots added of the Tsar talking impatiently to Rasmussen before we view the mining, and a similar conversation with Kurbsky (*How long before the attack?*) before the latter tries his cruel stratagem with the captives.

REEL FIVE

Goes straight on, beginning with the next shots in the scenario, Basmanov-father speaking to his son Fedka: *See there, Fyodor! See, son—*

But the whole episode of the delay in the explosion and the threatened execution of the gunners is omitted. From the two Basmanovs we go at once to the explosions (page 88) and then the assault, with Ivan's cry to aid Kurbsky.

Here, in both scenario and finished film, the Kazan episode ends. In the film, however, the embassies and homage (page 91) are omitted and we go straight on to the hushed corridors, where the scenario is followed exactly, down to Euphrosyne's ironical prayer: *And bringeth him also to the dust* . . .(page 93).

REEL SIX

Starts with the corridor colloquy between Euphrosyne and Kurbsky, *Well, Prince, always second?* . . . (page 93), and follows the scenario exactly to Malyuta's summons, *The Tsar commands* . . . (page 99).

REEL SEVEN

Omits the stately march to the bedchamber, headed by Euphrosyne, and the further line from the Livonian to Kurbsky. It goes straight to the bedchamber (page 100).

Again the film follows the scenario closely, down to Euphrosyne's cry: *All must kiss the cross to Tsar Vladimir!* (page 105).

REEL EIGHT

Here there is considerable improvement. Instead of Kurbsky bending over Ivan, looking closely at him, and then rather obscurely demonstrating that he is on Ivan's side by shooing out the boyars, thus earning Ivan's gratitude (page 106), the elements of the action are much more clearly divided.

Kurbsky goes up to the prostrate Ivan, looks closely at him, and then exchanges pregnant glances with Anastasia and leaves the bedchamber. He is followed by the boyars, led by Euphrosyne and Vladimir, who chant, *Glory to the boyar Tsar!*

Kurbsky pauses beneath the giant and watchful eye of an immense Byzantine-style mural of the Savior. As the others pass he muses, *The path to the throne . . . the path to the crown . . . which is it? Anastasia? Euphrosyne?*

Anastasia enters the corridor and tries to pass him. He seizes her:

Anastasia! Be mine—I shall protect thee from the boyars . . . be mine—I shall lead thee to the throne . . . be mine; together we shall rule the realm!

M.S.[1] Anastasia drags herself free and leaves the shot.

L.S.[2] Anastasia flees along the corridor. Kurbsky halts her.

KURBSKY:

Without thee life is not life, together with thee death not death . . .

M.S. Anastasia tears herself away.

C.U.[3] Anastasia and Kurbsky come into the shot.

KURBSKY:

Beside thee, to mount the

[1] Medium Shot.
[2] Long Shot.
[3] Close-up.

throne or scaffold were all one!

c.u. The Eye of the Savior.
Kurbsky (off screen):
. . . my Tsarina of Muscovy.

c.u. Anastasia and Kurbsky against the background of the image.
Anastasia:
It is not fitting, Prince, to bury before his death one yet alive.
Kurbsky draws back abruptly.

Kurbsky is horrified. *Does Ivan live?* he asks her. *God be thy Judge!* she replies. And Kurbsky, whispering over to himself Euphrosyne's words to him, *"With Ivan living Kurbsky cannot live,"* goes into the next chamber where Pimen, Euphrosyne, and Vladimir are waiting with the boyars for the oath of fealty.

To their bewilderment he runs to the lectern, takes the cross, and exclaims, in long shot:
In the name of the Father, the Son, and the Holy Ghost . . .
m.s. Pimen, Euphrosyne and Vladimir.
Kurbsky (off screen):
On the Holy Gospels I swear to serve truly and faithfully . . .

c.u. Kurbsky:
. . . the heir to the throne, the rightful Tsar of Muscovy . . .
c.u. Vladimir.
c.u. Kurbsky:
. . . Dmitry, son of Ioannis . . .
c.u. Pimen jumps up.

m.s. Euphrosyne recoils.
c.u. Vladimir looks on thunderstruck.
c.u. Kurbsky:
. . . and upon this I kiss the cross.
He kisses the cross.

In mid-shot Euphrosyne goes forward to tackle him, but before she can do so, Ivan enters, interrupting the scene with *The Holy Sacraments brought me succor* (page 106) and proceeding to the end of the scene as per scenario, with the now fully motivated gratitude to Kurbsky and the surprise promotion of Basmanov-father (page 107). The reel also ends here. Only the "Ocean-sea, Azure sea" motif slips away; this, with the loss of the prologue, disappears everywhere.

REEL NINE

Goes straight on with the plotting at the Staritskys' Mansion (page 107).

Here the correspondence between scenario and film is still exact, the only modification the suggestion from Pimen that to combat the Tsar's power they must oppose his campaigns and refuse contributions against Livonia. Thereupon the plan to make away with Anastasia comes not from Pimen, as in the scenario (page 109), but as an addendum from Euphrosyne, who at the same time undertakes it.

The next scene—Ivan and Nepeya—starts close to the scenario (page 109), but with Ivan's rage at a less violent level, and he is more specific about what he wants explained to Elizabeth by means of the chessmen (*. . . how her Eng-*

lish ships, avoiding the Baltic Sea, may reach us by the White Sea).

REEL TEN

Begins with Nepeya's exit (page 112). Follows the scenario to the poisoning and death of Anastasia (page 117), which ends the reel.

REEL ELEVEN

Omits the scene of "The Palace of Sigismund."

Begins with the scene in the Cathedral beside Anastasia's coffin (page 120) and continues right through to the end of the Cathedral as in scenario, with this differ-

ence: the tempo of the ending is much swifter. After Fedka Basmanov's exclamation, *You are right* (page 129), we go straight to the Tsar's speech about how he will utilize the prospective summons from the people to aid his cause, the torchbearers' entrance, and finish (page 131) without the jealous remark from Basmanov-father to his son (page 130), which really is part of the plot of the uncompleted half of Part Two.

REEL TWELVE

Instead of the scene of the cavalcade traversing Moscow's outskirts (pages 132-133), there is a rather flat interior scene in the Kremlin (was snow hard to come by in Alma-Ata?), where a clerk reads to boyars and people a letter telling of Ivan's purpose in quitting Moscow and an oprichnik tells them that if they want him back they must go and get him.

At the Alexandrov Liberty, the whole ceremony of the blasphemous oprichnik oath is omitted. We find Ivan huddled in a chair, Malyuta asking if he awaits a messenger from Moscow (page 134), and Nepeya arriving with his tidings. The parts of the oath on pages 134-135 being omitted, we simply hear the singing of the pilgrimage. Ivan goes out into the open to accept the pilgrimage's call and then orders:

> Saddle the horses, to gallop to
> Moscow (page 138)
> for the sake of the great Russian
> realm!

And the film ends there without the start of the ride back.

TALE TWO

MAIN, CREDIT, AND INTRODUCTORY TITLES

1. IVAN THE TERRIBLE
2. Tale No. 2: THE BOYARS' PLOT
3. *Author of the Scenario and Producer-Director*—S. M. Eisenstein
4. *Photography*—Andrei Moskvin
   Eduard Tisse
5. *Music*—Sergei Prokofiev
   Lyrics—Vladimir Lugovsky

The preceding credits appear against rolling black clouds and ornamental backgrounds, with the same musical opening as for Part One. The remaining credits are given orally over a background of appropriate scenes from Part One.

Fourteen shots of the coronation accompany a commentary—

> This is the tale of the struggle of Tsar Ivan, the struggle of the founder of the Muscovite State with the enemies of the unity of Russian soil.

—and the opening verse of the introductory song of Part One:

294

Black clouds
Are gathering;
Crimson blood
Bathes the dawn.
Cunning treason—
From the Boyars—
To royal power
Offers battle.

Then follow twenty-five shots identifying each of the principal characters while the commentary continues:

> In the part of Ivan the Terrible—Nikolai Cherkasov; the Tsar's Men: Malyuta Skuratov—Mikhail Zharov; Alexey Basmanov—Amvrosy Buchma; his son Fyodor Basmanov—Mikhail Kuznetsov; the Metropolitan of Moscow and all Rus, Philip—Andrei Abrikosov; the Bishop of Novgorod, Pimen —Alexander Mgebrov; Peter Volynets—Vladimir Balashov; Euphrosyne Staritsky, the Tsar's aunt—Serafima Birman; her son, Vladimir Staritsky— Pavel Kadochnikov; Prince Andrew Mikhailovich Kurbsky—Mikhail Nazvanov; King Sigismund of Poland—Pavel Massalsky.*

Twenty-four more shots from the first part provide the background to the spoken introduction:

> 1564 was the year of the creation of the "Men Apart" as a private bodyguard; the year in which Tsar Ivan betook himself to the Alexandrov Liberty; the year in which the people set out on a pilgrimage to the Tsar to fetch him back; the year of the wicked betrayal by Prince Kurbsky, who surrendered the Russian army to the Poles and went over to King Sigismund.

ACTION ANALYSIS

The most important changes in "Tale Two" are that it stops after the first eight sequences of the script of Part Two, and that sections omitted from Part One (Prologue and Palace of Sigismund) have been included to explain the situation and intrigues as they exist when "Tale Two" opens. Part One had set the stage of the struggle between Ivan, supported by the people, and the boyars, relying on hostile foreigners. The first half of Part Two in the script was originally meant to show that struggle in concentrated form and the second half to depict Ivan's march to victory. But by paring away so much that relates to what preceded and followed Part Two of the script, and isolating its internal plot, "Tale Two" is reduced from the central section of a drama of epic proportions to an intimate, almost claus-

---

* Omitted from this list: The boy Ivan—Eric Pyriev. The only changes in technician credits (given at the end of the film) appear to be that Safonova now partners Naumova as joint Costume Art Director; the Assistant Art Director is N. Kuzin; Second Assistant Director with Kuznetsova is now F. Soluyanov; Production Management staff is given as I. Soluyanov, I. Zakar, and A. Eidus; the choreographer is R. Zakharin. Production—Alma-Ata and Mosfilm Studios, 1943-6.

trophobic horror story of intensified power. At the same time, the fidelity of its sections to the original scenario is, despite trims, even more extraordinary than in Part One. It is only the balance that has changed.

REEL ONE

Begins with the Main Title, a reduced number of credits, and extracts from Part One to introduce the characters and summarize the situation up to the point at which the film begins.

The action starts with the Palace of Sigismund sequence from Part One (page 117), with the jesters removed. A long section making an ironic, topical parallel with the then contemporary (1941-1944) "crusade against the East" has been introduced into Sigismund's speech.* Also, Kurbsky, in reporting to the King the assistance he expects within Rus, names the Kolychev boyars (subsequently executed for treason by Malyuta).

Then come the opening sequences of the script of Part Two—The Outskirts of Moscow and The Hall of Audience—which are unchanged. The latter runs up to the designation of the oprichniks, ending this reel.

REEL TWO

Begins with the entry of Philip (page 145). Nearly to the end of this sequence (The Hall of Audience), the film proceeds almost exactly as in the script, except that the essentials of the Prologue are introduced as a flashback, while Ivan is crouching on his throne pleading with Philip (between pages 147 and 149) to gain Philip's sympathy and understanding. Ivan speaks over black clouds to introduce the flashback, saying, *From my youth I have experienced the hostility of the boyars toward the Grand Prince of Muscovy. After the death of my father they killed my mother . . .* The whole Prologue follows, except that the death of Telepnev-Obolensky is omitted and only the two principal boyars follow the boy Ivan into his bedchamber. Returning from the flashback, Ivan explains his purpose—to unify Russia—and his ideas of support from the people more explicitly than in the script, but Philip is unmoved and the scene continues as before until the Reel ends with the curse (page 150).

REEL THREE

The Hall of Audience sequence

---

* In place of the last four lines spoken by Sigismund on page 120:
  S.: *Set by God's will, Lithuania, Poland, Livonia stand to bar the way against the barbarous Rus and stay his entry into the family of the enlightened West!*
  (Polish lady [Anna Golshansky] interjects: *Muscovites eat babes alive!*)
  S. (continues): *Russia has fruitful lands, fat cattle, a soil whose womb is full of riches, a people suited to be serfs. But a strong man upon the Russian throne is to the European sovereigns—death! The Tsar we need is the weakling Vladimir Staritsky. The rebel boyars must have our support, Tsar's rule must vanish, feudal authority be reaffirmed. We'll break the unity of Ivan's Rus! This broken—against Muscovy we Christian kings shall lead a new crusade!*

has now reached page 151 and continues to its end with Philip's exit as in script, except that Eustace is omitted. Eustace hovers in the background of some of the long shots, but, as Philip does not present him, of course we do not notice him.

After Philip's departure, the sequence continues exactly as in script with the temptation by Malyuta, the Tsar's surrender to it, his conscience pangs and appeal to God, and the scene in Anastasia's bedchamber where Fedka acquaints him with the facts of Anastasia's death. The reel ends as the Tsar looks through the secret window to the courtyard (page 159).

REEL FOUR

Eustace having been dropped (after all, his story came to a climax in what was remaindered to Part Three and its beginning would only be an excrescence here), he does not appear in the execution scene. The execution scene is unchanged except for the fact that Malyuta is not stripped to the waist but clad in heavy furs against the cold, and the sentence-reading is much longer, detailing the traitors' names and accusing them directly of plotting with the King of Poland. After the execution, however, the action is speeded up. There is no waiting and discussing; Malyuta reports directly to the Tsar, and after the latter's line, *Too few*, we go straight to the Metropolitan's Cell. Not only is all of Eustace omitted, but the oprichniks' foray against the boyars for slaughter and loot is also missing—an omission that adds to the concentration and claustrophobia and, hence, the tension.

The Metropolitan's Cell sequence is unchanged, but there is a marked change in the development of the Fiery Furnace Play Sequence in the Cathedral. Instead of the exacerbation of Philip's mood by the news of Turuntay-Pronsky's death, we have the Tsar entering in high good humor with the Basmanovs, hearing with amusement their account of their looting expedition (and discomfiture when they tried it on Euphrosyne). Ivan is reminded by Fyodor of Euphrosyne's guilt in the murder of Anastasia. Stern at once, stopping Fyodor with a *Silence, Fedka, upon the great suspicion . . . God grant she be not guilty*, he then overhears the ambiguous singing of the martyrs and advances to meet Philip as on page 173. This ends the reel.

REEL FIVE

From the confrontation of Ivan and Philip the Cathedral Sequence proceeds unchanged to its end, except that the incident of the monks dropping the ornamental angel and the billowing flame do not occur. Perhaps Sergei Mikhailovich felt it was too much.

The sequence At the Staritskys', with Pimen and Peter, is unaltered and continues to the exit of Pimen (page 181), with which the reel ends. There is a small addendum: Euphrosyne puts her thought about the holy man—unspoken in the script—into words: *White cowl, black soul.*

REEL SIX

Still in the At the Staritskys' sequence, beginning with Vladimir's *Why are you pushing me to power?* and the bloodcurdling lullaby.

The whole sequence continues to its close with the sight of Peter, the invitation brought by Malyuta, his departure with Vladimir; all is exactly the same except for one significant change. The ending is immensely strengthened by the elimination of Euphrosyne's comprehension and frenzy (page 187). After the exit of the pair and Euphrosyne's double-meaning line about the robe thrown after them, she uncovers Malyuta's "gift," repeating her couplet: *The finger of God! Our cause prospers!* The fade-out comes sharply after she recognizes the cup and murmurs wonderingly, *Empty?*

REEL SEVEN

The first reel in color: blues with scarlets that have somewhat deteriorated to orange since they were photographed (but perhaps, considering wartime conditions, we are lucky that they have survived to any degree).*

The Feast sequence closely follows the script, right up to the command to dress the clown in the Tsar's robes, with which the reel ends. But, intensifying the claustrophobia, the boyars and Tartars present in the script are omitted. The incident of the elder Basmanov grumbling and being snubbed for his ambitions, which—like his pilfering in the omitted looting scene —is really a plant to prepare for the extermination of the Basmanov family in Part Three, was (rather surprisingly) retained. In its new context, it certainly does not disturb; instead, it helps to show the spectator that the Tsar is working to an end and far from being as tipsy as he pretends. This whole reel follows the script closely up to the top of page 197.

REEL EIGHT

The Feast continues, and with it the color.

There is one addition: an intensification of a climax by a qualitative change—a line instead of a visual image, spoken words instead of an unspoken thought (exactly like the substitution of Euphrosyne's

* Some critics have commented adversely on Eisenstein's use of color within a generally black-and-white film. The point should be made that this is by no means his first use of color—only of *color photography*. The flag at the masthead of the battleship "Potemkin" as it steams toward the fleet at the end of the film by that name was photographed white in order to be hand-painted red. Most contemporary copies lack that touch, partly because the generation of hand painters of separate celluloid frames has vanished from modern laboratories, but mainly because most Film Institutes do not know of it. In *The Old and the New*, the shot of fireworks that climaxes the grown-giant bull's charge upon the bedecked cow at the end of the Wedding of the Cow and the Bull should similarly be varicolored. Eisenstein would have regarded it as the worst kind of formalism to abstain from coloring a shot, part of a shot, or even a sequence that might be more effective in color merely on the ground that the rest of the film is in black and white.

lines for her acted thoughts at the close of both Reels Five and Six).* As Ivan watches Vladimir smile and reads his secret thoughts (page 197), not only do his eyes darken—as in the script—but he also gives a start and exclaims: *He likes it . . . the Polish hireling!* Then, instead of a bell ending the coronation masquerade and leading to the mock prayer, Ivan claps his hands—an action that is now also powerfully motivated.

At the close of the sequence, as the camera turns to follow the throng out of the hall toward the Cathedral, the color ceases suddenly; the resumed black and white appears, by illusionary contrast, almost silver and blue.

We spend longer with Vladimir dithering on the brink of entry into the Cathedral and the hooded throng shepherding him, pressing in on him. The action has been carefully intensified here, and inside the Cathedral also, where Vladimir's wavering advance seems to take an infinitude of time. But the line of development followed in the script is quite unchanged, and the only new element is that Malyuta, with narrowed eyes, watches the assassin as he steps from pillar to pillar. The singing by the oprichniks of their blasphemous parody—the Fearful Oath—which takes place both here and at the end of the sequence (in the next reel) lacks the dramatic force of repetition because it has been used in none of the earlier places foreseen in the script and

retains only its intrinsic quality as a hymn from Hell.

The reel ends with the stabbing, immediately before the shot of the actual stab (page 203).

REEL NINE

Beginning with the stab and a cry (not in script) from the victim.

The scene in the film again follows the script development closely, but again there is a wonderful touch of intensification. As Ivan (who must seem to Euphrosyne a doppelgänger) slowly advances through the opened ranks of the oprichniks (page 205), Euphrosyne is frozen as a rabbit before a stoat and finally, as he stops, takes a tiny step to touch him with her outstretched arm and find him real before bending down to peer at her son. All this has been developed from the single script line: "Euphrosyne has given a shudder."

An interesting minor change, the significance of which was lost with the disappearance of Part Three, is that the Tsar-Peter scene has now been placed in front of the great fresco of the Last Judgment. This is typical Eisenstein "double blow" narrative technique—the spot where one enemy is spared is the same place where later Ivan confesses to countless enemies not spared.

The only major change lies in the ending, obviously dictated by the separation of the second part into two. The ending attempts to do what the whole framework of the second part was designed to do

* The process by which Eisenstein actually arrived at this type of solution is described in Nikolskaya's paper, "Sketches on the Margins."

when Eisenstein originally wrote it:
put this horror story into perspective as part of the Tsar's noble
struggle for the unity of Rus and
relate it topically to the U.S.S.R.'s
situation in the midst of World
War II. Of course it does not do
this properly, but it was highly necessary to try, given the extraction of
this section to make a film on its
own. One can only say that it
makes the best of a (formalistically)
bad job.

The text of the mock hymn sung
by the choir of oprichniks as the
procession moves away does not follow the script (page 208); instead,
the film uses the verse (lines 20-24
and 27-28) on page 134 of Part One.
Also, one line of the oath—the last
—is spoken by Tsar Ivan, who has
fallen to his knees and crossed himself as the singing began. There is
no return to Peter and his coins;
instead, there is a fade-out and then
a fade-in with a grim blue-and-red-

colored scene of Tsar Ivan seated
on a throne surrounded by the
Tsar's Men. He pronounces a solemn summing up (the first two
sentences are actual quotes from
the historical Tsar Ivan and occur
in his letters to Kurbsky):

*A Tsar must ever be
watchful that to the good
goes mercy and mildness
and, to the evil—wrath and
torment. Else he nor
should be, nor is, a Tsar!
Today the Moscow foes of
the unity of Russian soil
are vanquished—my hands
are free! And hencefor-
ward the sword of right-
eousness shall flash against
those who encroach from
without upon the majesty
of the Russian State. We
shall not yield Rus to
shame!*

And that is the final fade-out.

I. M.

300

MY DRAWINGS*

by Sergei M. Eisenstein

In '12† Moscow, they say, was suddenly set on fire from four sides at once.

Rus, from end to end, shall blaze with flames of insurrection! the traitor Kurbsky cries in the *Ivan* scenario.

And in the overture, prophetic voices chant through the roar of the rolling thunder:

> *On the bones of its foes*
> *From the four corners of*
> *the earth*

The Russian realm . . .
Rises.

To set Moscow on fire exactly that way or to do things exactly as the historic Kurbsky put it is not easy.

But there is one process which, inevitably, just like that—at once, simultaneously, instantly—starts from all corners, from every side. That is —the process of film creation.

A finished film is a coordinated and homologized assemblage of the

---

* This is an introduction written by the author for a collection of his *Ivan* sketches planned for publication in 1943, while he was still making the film and at about the same time the scenario was published. It does not seem to have appeared until later.
† 1812.

most diverse means of expression and action.

The historical content of the theme, the scenario plot and the general development of the drama, the bringing to life of the imagined image and the acting of the live actor, the rhythm of the editing and the plastic structure of the shot; music, sound, noise; mise-en-scène and the reciprocal play of the interwoven movements; color and the tonal composition of the dialogue, etc.

In a successful production all this is welded into a unity.

One law regulates all. And the seeming chaos of incommensurable, separate spheres and measurements is combined into a single regulated whole.

But how do you make this future whole come into being, when you approach the task of giving embodiment to the chosen theme?

Like the burning of Moscow.

From all sides at once.

And from the most unexpected and unforeseen corners.

So, internally, with the separate spheres of the assemblage.

So also in the relationship of the spheres to the whole.

The dramatic theme, the essence of the film about Tsar Ivan, was originally sparked into life with the idea for a scene that comes somewhere in the middle of Part Two.

This was the first episode that arose in my imagination—the episode setting the stylistic key—the Confession Sequence. Where and when it came into my head I can no longer be certain.

I remember, however, that it was the first.

Second to come was the Prologue: the Death of Helena Glinsky.

It happened in a box at the Bolshoy Theater.

The first jotting down of the scene was on the back of a ticket.

The epic color of the script sprang from the episode that arose third: Candle over Kazan.

It came suddenly after reading a song about the taking of Kazan.

So, internally, with the separate spheres.

In the movement of the drama:

First—a scene somewhere near the end.

Then—suddenly the Prologue.

Next—unexpectedly the middle.

Likewise in the biography of the image:

Here's a scene from age.

Then suddenly—childhood.

Next—the flower of youth.

So also with the separate spheres themselves.

One you may visualize as a vivid slice of life.

A second you act.

A third you hear.

For a fourth you see a shot.

A fifth you feel as an already edited sequence.

A sixth as a chaos of colored blotches.

And on scraps of paper arise now a fragment of dialogue; now a plan of the positioning of the actors on the floor; now an instruction to the art director about softened edges for the vaulted ceilings; now one for the associate director on the rhythm of an as yet unwritten scene; now a suggestion to the composer proposing that the theme of the "Terrible" be constructed from four interwoven leitmotifs; now one for the lyric writer on the tone of a ribald song or a couplet for the future Foma and Yeroma.*

Now, all the words and plans suddenly discarded, the scraps of paper begin to be filled with sketches.

Without concrete visualization of people in action, activity, reciprocal positioning, it is impossible to write down their behavior on paper.

Before your eyes they march continuously.

Sometimes so palpably that it seems as though you could put them down on paper without opening your eyes.

It will be their task to appear before the camera in one year, two, three.

Let us strive to commit the essence of them to paper.

So are born the sketches.

They are not illustrations to the scenario.

Still less—embellishments to a book.

They are sometimes a first impression of the feeling of a scene which is then transcribed from them and written down in the scenario.

Sometimes—they make it easier, already at this preparatory stage, to watch the behavior of the characters as they come into your mind.

Sometimes—they are a concentrated record of the feeling the

* e.g., p. 267.

scene must give rise to; most often, of the search for it.

Such searches are indeed endless, twenty times over breaking up the scenes into different courses of movement, succession of episodes, changes of the actor's lines within an episode.

Sometimes—in the future scene as shot there will be nothing whatsoever of the original sketches.

Sometimes—the rough jotting seems two years hence almost to come to life.

Sometimes a whole pile of roughly sketched out drawings does not even get as far as the scenario.

Sometimes the scene never gets outside the covers of the working script.

But sometimes, also, a design for set construction arises from these drafts.

Sometimes this or that aspect of makeup or of costume.

Sometimes they determine the actual form of the future shot.

Sometimes they turn out to be the model for the perspective in which the actor's movements will be seen.

Least often are these sketches finished, mostly are they transient, most often of all comprehensible only to the author.

An example of them, chosen from hundreds of scribblings: three perspectives of Ivan in the Confession Sequence, in front of the fresco of the Last Judgment.

Participants in the process of visual and dramatic embodiment of the theme, these jottings can probably also serve to help the reader get a fuller feeling of the author's purpose, so far only set down on paper.

Two thousand of their colleagues still lie in their portfolios.

Those reproduced here crave the reader's indulgence:

Visual stenograms—they claim to be nothing more.

Alma-Ata, October 1943

From SKETCHES ON THE MARGINS*

by V. Nikolskaya

. . . Now let us turn to another, yet more important stage of the creative process—the working out of the shooting directly before going on the floor.

In front of us is a most precious document, Eisenstein's own copy of the *Ivan the Terrible* scenario. Its appearance alone would attract attention. The typed sheets, slightly yellowed by time, are bound between covers of a handsome cloth shot through with silver and gold. Its fancy pattern shimmeringly repeats various shades—from pale yellow to dark green.

As we study the penciled notes on the margins and compare with them both the roughed-out *mise-en-scènes*† and the drawings made as preparatory sketches of what the director meant later to shoot, we realize that what we have here is the work done immediately before actual production.

What is it, then, that occurs in the visual imagination of the director before he goes on the floor?

---

* See Bib. (32). The copy of the script described, that used personally by Eisenstein and now in the possession of the widow of Moskvin, his cameraman for the interiors, is evidently an already slightly revised version of the first printed scenario.

† *Mise-en-scène*—the plan of the positioning of the actors in a scene, just as they would be placed and moved on the stage in the theater, is, in Soviet cinema practice, worked out first, and the breaking down into shots and special technical "film" handling is worked out subsequently.

What is the process of his search for the best choice and composition of scenes and shots? What was changed in the screenplay and why?

Looking for the answers to these questions, let us examine the director's revision of certain episodes in a climactic sequence of Part One—the illness of Ivan the Terrible. Here, in a bitter struggle for the throne, the characters of those who support and those who oppose the dying Tsar are completely revealed. This section of the film was made more and more precise by Eisenstein, a process which continued right up to shooting.

While the director was satisfied originally with having mastered the general idea of these episodes, the nearer he got to shooting, the deeper became his search for solution of the problems that they raised, the more specific became his drawings, notes, plans, and diagrams in the margins and on the blank backs of the opposite scenario pages. One of these diagrams (Fig. 1) is a plan of the mise-en-scène and movements for the scene of the Tsar receiving extreme unction.* It follows the scenario action exactly and works out the latter's realization in detail. The route of the monks' procession (their original positions provisionally marked according to a code) is indicated by a dotted line with an arrow showing its direction. The positions of the

* See p. 94.

Figure 1

characters are labeled: "Tsar," "Dmitry," and "Anastasia." The place intended by the director for the Metropolitan, Pimen, is marked by a cross. A separate drawing illustrates the moment when the dying Tsar is handed a candle by one of the monks. Beside it Eisenstein has jotted down a note that the remaining participants in the procession must pass around the giver of the candle to continue their route.

At the same time as he was busy with these important aspects of filming the scene, Eisenstein did not ignore small details. Between sketch and diagram are typical notes: "N.B. Do two door casings (one, painted on the wall, the other covering it over). Icon niche—do it with a cupboard: when the icon is removed—the cupboard is visible. Then the bed can be 'twisted.'"

And here is another note. "N.B. During the extreme unction, no Malyuta. M.* below on the stairs for buildup."

This last note foresees the following development of the action; the place which the director has assigned Malyuta enables the latter to overhear the private conversation in which Euphrosyne Staritsky asks Kurbsky whom he will pledge to serve after Ivan's death.

No less carefully worked out is the scene of the procession of the boyars into Ivan the Terrible's bedchamber and its continuation to the bed of the Tsar, where the latter calls on them in the event of his death to kiss the cross to his son. This scene also has a diagram of its own (Fig. 2). Of special interest

* i.e., Malyuta.

here are shooting instructions for the cameraman.

In addition to notes beside the diagram of the mise-en-scène, the actions of the characters are also made more precise in pencil jottings on the mimeographed text of the screenplay. Thus, for example, after the lines, "Defiantly gaze back at Ivan, Euphrosyne Staritsky and her son Vladimir," * is added in Eisenstein's handwriting: "Euph. indicates Vl-r as *h e i r*." This addition was used in the film itself, as was another on this paper, where, after Ivan's words, "Kiss the cross to . . . Dmitry . . . ," † Eisenstein penciled a note for Vladimir to turn in fear to his mother, who then thrusts him forward.

On the same page lines are drawn round the words: "Not for my sake./ Not for my son:/ but for the Russian land [altered to 'unity of' the Russian land in E's. handwriting—I.M.] I beg you." The passage is moved to the foot of the page. This transposition is easy to justify: these important words clarify the point of the scene, and if they came earlier they might escape the attention of the spectator. Now they conclude the scene and thereby sum up the whole conception.

With equal care, Eisenstein found the right expression for the access of wrath that seizes Ivan when the boyars refuse to kiss the cross to Tsarevich Dmitry.

In the original text (Fig. 3, script page 58, ll. 22, 23) the Tsar fell on the boyars with a resounding curse, thus:

* P. 100 and, in Fig. 2., ll. 18, 19.
† In Fig. 2, ll. 23, 24.

For this, for all time
accursed be! *

Eisenstein marked this text with a pencil, put a colon against it, and wrote this modification, underlining the word Russian:

Of Russian *soil betrayers, for this,*
for all time accursed be!

But this, too, failed to satisfy the author. On the opposite blank page he attempts to find a still more expressive quality for the phrase, with added directions for the actor. Now Ivan's line is tried like this:

In horror: *Of Russian soil betrayers . . . for this for all time accursed be . . .*

* P.,102.

To full height on the bed: *For this, for all time, accursed* be!

We find that, when the film was shot, assembled from all the previous versions of the passage, Ivan's speech went like this:

For this, for all time
accursed be,
of Russian soil betrayers.

And Eisenstein's stage direction that the actor must pronounce this concluding part of the speech standing at his full height on the bed is the way it is done in the film.

No less persistently has Eisenstein sought a final text for the closing lines of Anastasia's speech. Her last two lines in the text on the

Figure 2

same page (Fig. 3) originally ran like this:

> . . . *hating one the other,*
> *foreign governance*
> *you'll serve.**

This construction of the passage did not satisfy Eisenstein. Beneath the typed text he formulated the general idea that the passage should convey, in the following line:

> *whate'er betide you'll not be free*
> *—only to worse masters slaves*
> *you'll be!*

Next Eisenstein made the original version more precise with the following, dated "26th March 1944," inserted in pencil:

> *Not native soil, but . . .*

This is what the passage now looked like:

> . . . *hating one the other,*
> *not native soil, but foreign*
> *governance*
> *you'll serve!*

The final version was drafted after Eisenstein had worked out the visual form for Anastasia's delivery of the entire speech. Facing the text page is a drawing (Fig. 3) of the Tsarina holding up Tsarevich Dmitry. This is how Eisenstein sees Anastasia delivering the first part

---

* In the printed scenario (p. 103) the last four words of the first line form a single line.

Figure 3

of it (*Only in* Dmitry—his son—lies salvation—I.M.). Right of that she is drawn pressing her son to her heart and delivering the last part of her speech, now written below as:

> . . . *not native soil with
> faith, truth shall you serve,
> but strangers' slaves you'll
> be!*

In the actual film this wording is slightly revised:

> . . . *not native soil, faith
> and truth
> shall you serve, but unto
> foreign
> governance slaves you'll be!*

All these experiments plainly testify how carefully Eisenstein polished every phrase, trying to find the words and combinations that should most briefly and deeply, beautifully and resonantly convey what he wanted to express. The more the conflict grows in this sequence of the struggle for the throne, the more restless grows Eisenstein's mind under the stress of creation.

The dramatic confrontation of the two mothers whose sons are the rival claimants to the Russian throne—Anastasia and Euphrosyne—fully engrosses Eisenstein's attention.

The text of this part of the sequence is worked over and changed again and again. The original text no longer satisfies the director. Ruthlessly he strikes out whatever is superfluous. New versions enrich the text. Notes and remarks addressed to the actors and cameraman appear. The exact revision of the wording is accompanied by roughs of diagrams, drafts of mise-en-scènes, sketches of shots. Pages 59 and 60 of the script* (Figs. 4, 5) are literally spattered with evidence of the strain of the creative process.

The revision by the director of these scenes bears out Eisenstein's own phrase for his creative process: "from every quarter, from every side" †—from the sides of drama, acting, graphic representation, as well as music and sound.

Following Anastasia's appeal to the boyars, Euphrosyne appeals to them in her turn. Originally her words ran as follows (Fig. 4, script page 59, ll. 13, 14):

> *Never shall the boyars, glorious,
> of ancient lineage, lie
> beneath the heels of Glinsky—
> Zakharins.‡*

Trying to make Euphrosyne's lines more concrete in idea, Eisenstein adds to the first the word "stout" and to the second the words "heirs of Ivan."

Then, for the last word "Ivan," Eisenstein substitutes "the prince of Muscovy." Now the idea of the lines has become clearer and the form of its expression more definite —the speech has acquired completeness and definiteness and revealed its sociological meaning. To appreciate this, read the speech thus amended.

> *Never shall the boyars, stout, of
> ancient lineage, lie
> beneath the heels of Glinsky—
> Zakharin
> heirs to the prince of Muscovy.*

* Pp. 102-103.
† *See* "My Drawings," p. 301.
‡ *See* p. 104; the line in the screenplay as printed does not mention Anastasia's family.

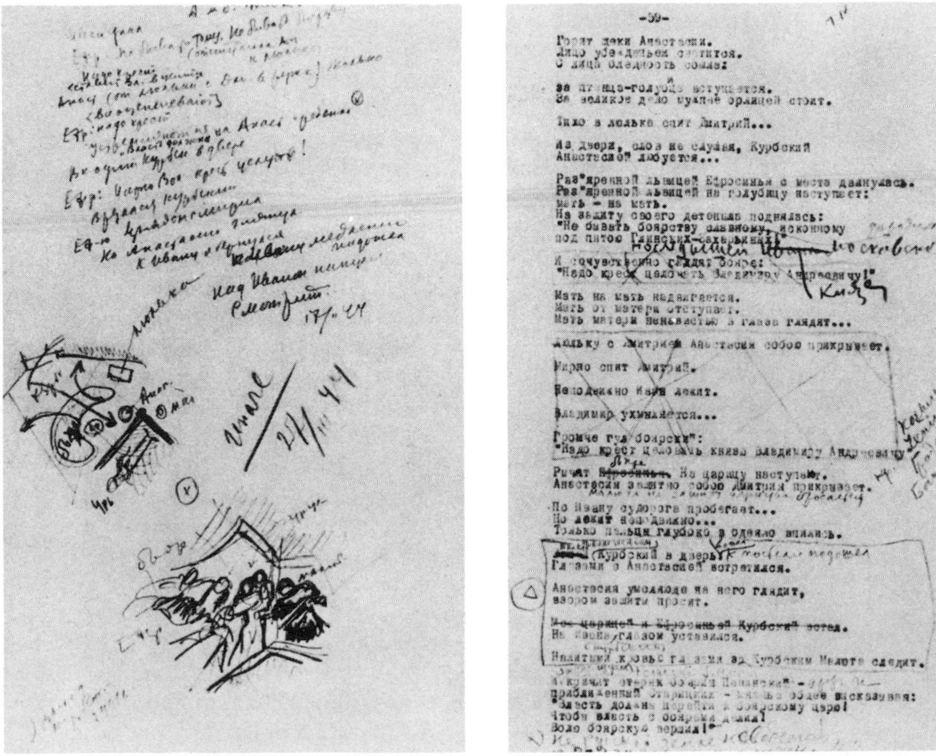

Figure 4

This is how, or, more correctly, almost how, the spectator hears the speech in the film. Evidently, in the process of shooting, something even more exact was hit upon: instead of *the heels of Glinsky–Zakharin heirs to the prince of Muscovy*, the phrase spoken is *the heel of a Glinsky–Zakharin heir to the prince of Muscovy*. The line, now rendered as specific as possible, thus points directly to Tsarevich Dmitry.

The next two lines of the script are struck out, and the reaction of the boyars that they describe is, following a still further cut, deferred to a later place (Fig. 4, script page

59, l. 26), where it replaces an action of Euphrosyne. The sentence *Euphrosyne snarls* is now changed to *The boyars snarl*.

One line later Eisenstein writes in:

"Malyuta plunges to the defense of the Tsarina."

What is the purpose of all these seemingly insignificant changes? The passages formerly included and now removed—shots showing the reaction of those present—threatened to blur the growth of the developing action: the furious confrontation of the two mothers. Now the distractions are removed, the reaction of the boyars becomes, as it were, a sort of closing Greek Chorus comment on the confrontation, and its undesirable tinge of a mere editing detail is now eliminated. The final action of all participants in the scene has been developed to a unity, resounding like a mighty chord:

The boyars snarl. They bear down on the Tsarina.

Anastasia defensively protects Dmitry with her body,

Malyuta plunges to the defense of the Tsarina.

Notice also Eisenstein's penciled scribbling at this point in the margin of the scenario page:

C.U. Kolychevs
Chepurnoy
Grodsky
Batzman

This is a reminder of the necessity to fix certain characters and protagonists in the scene with closeups. Even a detail of this kind Eisenstein certainly did not wish to leave to a last-minute, impromptu choice, where chance might play too great a role; still less could he look on the selection of close-ups as a matter of indifference.

Further precision has been brought to Kurbsky's entry into the bedchamber.*

From the penciled notes on the blank script page (Fig. 4) it is clear that the director at this stage is interested not only in *what* the character does but in *how* he does it. At the same time he works out

the mise-en-scène in exact detail. Now Kurbsky no longer simply enters; he "enters briskly." The instruction is inserted that Kurbsky "comes up to the Tsar's bed."

Kurbsky is no exception; all the rest of the participants' actions in the scene are now seen by the director equally palpably and clearly. Their behavior and changes of position are indissolubly linked in his imagination with the dialogue. These notes on the page facing script page 59 show this (Fig. 4). They are in a hastily penciled scribble. Some of them are not written out in full. Others are very much abbreviated indeed. Evidently the author could not wait to put down on paper all the flow of ideas, images, and visualizations that came pouring in on him. The writing is dated "17th February, 1944."

Little more than a month passes and in clear firm handwriting Eisenstein laconically notes: "Otherwise 27. III. 44."

Now the same scene is seen by the director rather differently and—this is the main thing—still more exactly. Now in place of verbal descriptions he has diagrams and drawings.

The positioning of the characters becomes absolutely clear. The places of Ivan the Terrible, Anastasia, Euphrosyne, Malyuta, the boyars, and Kurbsky are exactly marked on the diagram. An arrow crossing the diagram in the center

---

* This and the following passage, describing Kurbsky's hesitation between Anastasia and Euphrosyne, have clearly been much developed since the originally published screenplay (*see* pp. 104-105). The new scene between Kurbsky and Anastasia (*see* p. 290-292) was obviously a part of this development.—I.M.

of the page shows the direction of Kurbsky's approach to the Tsar's bedside.

The diagram is given precision by a drawing, below, that excellently conveys the tension and dynamism of the scene. The cross on the left above the drawing marks the point of Kurbsky's appearance in the bedchamber.

Having thought out the final part of the scene, Eisenstein somewhat alters the succession of proceedings in its developing action. He draws a line around one passage in the text* toward the bottom of the

* See p. 104, ll. 19-25.

page (Fig. 4, script page 59, ll. 31-37), marks it with a triangle, and moves it to near the top of the next script page (Fig. 5, script page 60, between ll. 6 and 7).

This next page undergoes important revision where (ll. 11-14) it describes the final behavior of Kurbsky.† Eisenstein tries to strengthen the motif of the prince's shrewd maneuvering against the background of complicated court intrigue. To this end, he completely rewrites the old text here and replaces it by a new one (see Fig. 5, left-hand side, which is the back of script page 59).

† See p. 105, ll. 10-13. What Eisenstein has done in the changes is to bring together and expand all the material of Kurbsky's hesitation.

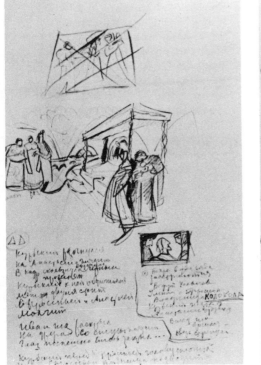

Figure 5

To make it easier for the reader to get the full implication of Eisenstein's changes here, we shall quote this handwritten passage in full:

Kurbsky is irresolute,
he looks at Anastasia,
in the shot he has glanced at the black profile of Euphrosyne,
Kurbsky has turned toward the latter,
he stands betwixt the two,
Euphrosyne and Anastasia,
he says nothing.

(This moment is recorded in a small drawing appearing directly above' the last part of the handwritten text.)

Ivan has opened his eye.
From behind he looks on his friend.
The eye has promptly closed anew . . .
Kurbsky has bowed his head to Euphrosyne,
To Euphrosyne Umnoy* leads Vladimir.

The boyars in two rows
make way,
as Umnoy Kolychev leads
to Euphrosyne
Vladimir.
Kurbsky his eye from
Anastasia has torn away,
he has hastened after them. . . .
The door has shut with a bang.

It would be hard to exaggerate the significance of this new version. It has sharply increased the dramatic impact of the scene. Further-more, the plot point has been given much more concrete visual expression. It is specially noteworthy that there appears in it an instruction designed to strengthen its emotional force by means of sound—the ringing of the bell (see the separate note in strong capitals, "BELL," near the bottom of the left-hand page in Fig. 5).†

The little crossed-out drawing at the top left of the same page was meant to fix the moment of Euphrosyne's assailing Anastasia. But the solution he drew there displeased Sergei Mikhailovich. He twice redrew the scene (not on this page) and still came back to it. Below, the author's attention has changed to the moment when Euphrosyne and the boyar Umnoy Kolychev led Vladimir Staritsky to Ivan's bed. The main drawing on this page is devoted to it. The right-hand part of the drawing, near the Tsar's bed, shows Anastasia and Malyuta, with the child Dmitry in the latter's arms. One arrow shows the direction of movement of Vladimir; another, coming from the depths of the bedchamber, marks the path of Kurbsky. Kurbsky himself is not shown in this drawing because at this precise moment he is outside the confines of the bed-chamber—in the adjacent royal chapel. This we infer from the script line in the text, which reads, "Kurbsky has been waiting in the chapel antechamber . . ." The last-minute, penciled annotation under this line (Fig. 5, script page 60,

---

* Umnoy ("The Wise")—the elder of the Kolychevs.
† The "BELL" occurs just after the word "Vladimir" in the last section above. But note the similar role of the slamming of the door at the end.

l. 25) defines the inner mood of the prince; Eisenstein writes that he looks at the icon and guesses to whom he should do homage if he is to avoid making a mistake on his road to the throne. Eisenstein's linked pencil marks go on, and, near the bottom of the page, he condenses the entire drama in progress with a brief listing:

Anastasia?
Euphrosyne?
Anastasia! *

All the detailed polishing and correction of the text here was carried out without any changes when the scene was shot.

Alterations took place in several other lines in this part of the sequence. For example, Euphrosyne's cry, *All must kiss the cross to Tsar*

* See p. 290.

Vladimir, has become more commanding: *All kiss the cross to Tsar Vladimir!* (*see* Fig. 5, l. 4).

There has also been a change in the dialogue of Kurbsky's courting of Anastasia.

Originally this ran:

Be mine—I shall lead Dmitry to the throne.

Be mine—beside thee I shall rule the realm.

This was later corrected to the following:

Be mine—I shall lead thee to the throne.

Be mine—together we shall rule the realm!†

The examples quoted above are only a tiny fraction of the huge material of Eisenstein's creative legacy still awaiting investigation. . . .

† See p. 290.

SELECT BIBLIOGRAPHY

Writings by S. M. Eisenstein

1, 2. NOT COLOURED BUT IN COLOUR.[1] There is a reference to *Ivan* in this article, which was written in 1940 and published in English as pages 114-119 in the volume *Notes of a Film Director*[2] by Eisenstein, issued by the Foreign Languages Publishing House, Moscow, n.d. (1957), and Lawrence & Wishart, London, 1959.

3. IVAN GROZNY (IVAN THE TERRIBLE). The report of a Party production Conference at Mosfilm studio, including extracts from a speech by Eisenstein on the work in progress on the film, published in the newspaper *Vechernaya Moskva*, Moscow, June 1941.

4. IVAN GROZNY. A full analysis of the portrait of Ivan in the cinema, published in the newspaper *Literatura i Iskusstvo*, Moscow, July 4, 1942.

5. IVAN GROZNY. A variant of the same article published in *VOKS* (All-Union Society for Cultural Relations) *Bulletin*, Moscow, 1942, No. 7/8.

6. IVAN GROZNY. A discussion of the same subject published in the newspaper *Trud*, Moscow, Aug. 20, 1942.

7. PEREPISKA (CORRESPONDENCE) S. PROKOFIEVA I S. EISENSTEINA. In this article in the magazine *Sovietskaya Muzyka*, Moscow, April 1961

(No. 4), the letters from Eisenstein dated 1942-1946, which appear on pages 109-114, contain references to Eisenstein's collaboration with the composer on *Ivan*.

8, 9. Moi Risunki (My Drawings).[8] An introduction written in 1943 for the catalogue of an exhibition of *Ivan* drawings then projected; eventually printed as pages 207-212 of the anthology *Mosfilm, Vypusk I, Rabot nad Filmom* (*Work on Film, Mosfilm Issue No. 1*),[9] published by Gosizdat Iskusstvo, Moscow, 1959. (Here translated into English as our pages 301-304). See also 22.

10. Ivan Grozny. The screenplay, first published in the magazine *Novy Mir*, Moscow, October/November 1943 (No. 10/11), and as an illustrated book by Goskinoizdat, Moscow, 1944. (The latter is substantially the text here translated into English as our pages 21-281).

11-14. How we filmed "Ivan the Terrible."[11] In a Regisseur's Laboratory: 1. The First Vision.[12] 2. On the Lot.[13] Number 11, on the screen treatment; number 12, on the sketches; number 13, on the shooting—the last two illustrated and all three in English, published in *Cinema*, the Film Chronicle of VOKS, Moscow, February 1945.[14] The last two were reprinted (without illustrations), under the general title "Notes from a Director's Laboratory" and with No. 2 retitled "Facing the Camera" as pages 261-265 of *Film Form*, edited by Jay Leyda, published by Harcourt Brace, New York, 1949; Dobson Books, London, 1951; and Meridian Books, New York, 1957.

15. Nasha Rabota nad Filmom (Our Work on the Film). An article describing the work on Part One of the film, published in the newspaper *Izvestia*, Moscow, Feb. 4, 1945.

16. Krupneishy Gosudarstvenny Deyatel (A Foremost Statesman). On the image of Ivan as depicted in Part One, published in the magazine *Ogonyok*, Moscow, 1945, No. 9/10, page 14.

17, 18. P-R-K-F-V[17] (1946). An article by Eisenstein on the composer, with reference to their collaboration on *Ivan*, printed in English as pages 149-167 of *Notes of a Film Director* (see 2). It originally formed the introduction to *Sergei Prokofiev, His Musical Life*, by Israel V. Nesteyev,[18] published in Russian by Gosmuzykalnoyeizdat, Moscow, 1957, and in English by Knopf, New York, 1946, which contains many other references to their collaboration.

19. O Filme "Ivan Grozny." Letter to the editor of the newspaper *Kultura i Zhizn*, Moscow, Oct. 20, 1946, analyzing the ideological and artistic errors of "Tale Two" in acceptance of the Central Committee strictures (see 28).

20. Stereoscopic Films (1947-48). There are references to *Ivan* in this article, published in English as

pages 129-137 of *Notes of a Film Director* (see 2).

21. COLOUR FILM (1948). There is reference to *Ivan* in this article, published in English as pages 119-129 of *Notes of a Film Director* (see 2). E. was writing this article late at night and had just written the words: "So I shall give a short description of how the colour sequence was constructed in *Ivan the Terrible*," when he died of a sudden heart attack.

22. RISUNKI / DESSINS / DRAWINGS. A major collection of drawings in colour and black and white (text in Russian, French and English), published by Gosizdat Iskusstvo, Moscow, 1961. The volume includes the article listed as 8 (under the title "A Few Words on My Drawings") and some thirty pages of *Ivan* sketches and photos.

Writings by other authors
23. *Alexandrov, G. V.*, SERGEI EISENSTEIN'S "IVAN THE TERRIBLE." A general article and recollections published in the newspaper *Sovietskaya Kultura*, Moscow, Aug. 30, 1958.

24. *Bachelis, Ilya*, THE FIRST EXPERIMENT IN PRODUCING A FILM TRAGEDY. An analysis of the style of Part One, published in English in *Cinema*, the VOKS Film Chronicle (see 14).

25. *British Film Institute*, IVAN THE TERRIBLE. A leaflet containing a general summary and credits of the U.K. reissue of Part One, published as *B.F.I. Records of the Film No. 2* by the B.F.I., London, n.d. (1946).

26, 27. *Cherkasov, N.*, NOTES OF A SOVIET ACTOR.[26] References to his work with Eisenstein on *Ivan* occur on pages 103-106, 161, 162, 166 and 174 of the English-language edition of this book, issued by the Foreign Languages Publishing House, Moscow, n.d. (1957). The original Russian edition was published in 1953.

V TEATRE I V KINO (IN THE THEATER AND THE CINEMA).[27] A chapter in this book for children, comprising pages 82-86, deals with "The Taking of Kazan." It was published by Gosizdat Detskoy Literatury, Moscow, 1961.

28. C.P.S.U. (B.)* *Central Committee*, O KINOFILME "BOLSHAYA ZHIZN" (ON THE FILM "THE GREAT LIFE"). This directive, dated Sept. 4, 1946, and originally published as pages 50-53 of the magazine *Bolshevik*, Moscow, August 1946, contains the derogatory reference to "Tale Two" that led to the postponement of its public showing until 1959. The directive is reprinted as pages 575-576 of *O Partiinoy i Sovietsky Pechati, Sbornik Dokumentov* (*Party and Soviet Press Statements, a Collection of Documents*), issued by Izdateltsvo *Pravda*, Moscow, 1954.

29. *Marshall, H.*, (*trans.*), "IVAN THE TERRIBLE," A FILM SCENARIO. A translation of Part One and the

---

* Communist Party of the Soviet Union (Bolsheviks).

earlier section of Part Two (publication was not completed) in the magazine *Life and Letters*, London, 1945 (XI-XII), 1946 (I-IV, V-VII).

30, 31. *Montagu, I.*, EISENSTEIN'S "IVAN THE TERRIBLE."[30] A general article on Part One, published in the magazine *Our Time*, London, July 1945.

EISENSTEIN'S "IVAN THE TERRIBLE."[31] An illustrated booklet containing a general examination, credits and reproductions of stills from "Tale Two," published by Eurap, London, n.d. (1960).

32. *Nikolskaya, V.*, RISUNKI NA POLYAKH (SKETCHES ON THE MARGINS). An article containing an analysis, in its first half, of the drawings for *Alexander Nevsky*, and, in its second half, of notes, corrections and production sketches on the margins of Eisenstein's own copy of the *Ivan* script (now in the possession of the widow of Andrei Moskvin), both illustrated. The latter half forms pages 219-236 of *Work on Film, Mosfilm Issue No. 1* (see 9). (It is here translated into English as our pages 305-315.)

33. *Seton, M.*, EISENSTEIN. This "psychological" biography contains a summary and a highly imaginative and improbable interpretation of the *Ivan* film on pages 411-442. Published by the Bodley Head, London, 1952 and Grove Press, New York, 1960.

34. *Sokolova, Natalya*, U ISTOKOV FILMA (AT THE SOURCES OF THE FILM). A description of Eisenstein's home, the sketches, etc. (Illustrated), with references to *Ivan*, forming pages 213-218 of *Work on Film, Mosfilm Issue No. 1* (see 9).

35. *Vishnevsky, Vsevolod*, THE FILM "IVAN THE TERRIBLE." An excellent general article on Part One, published in the newspaper *Pravda*, Moscow, Jan. 29, 1945.

36. *Yurenyev, R.*, EISENSTEIN. "IVAN GROZNY" VTORAYA SERIYA (PART Two). A very full, and by far the best, account of Eisenstein's work on *Ivan*, the hitch over "Tale Two," and what happened subsequently. Comprises pages 139-176 of *Voprosy Kino Iskusstva, Vypusk 5 (Questions of Film Art, Issue 5)*, published by Izdateltsvo Akademii Nauk S.S.S.R., Moscow, 1961.

In preparation: in Paris—an illustrated volume on the exhibition by the Cinemathèque of the Eisenstein drawings for *Ivan*; in Moscow —by the All-Union Publishing House of Soviet Composers, the piano score of Prokofiev's *Ivan* Oratorio, arranged by A. Stasyevich, with lyrics in English (translated by Herbert Marshall) as well as Russian, and later the full orchestral score.

The abbreviation "n.d." in these listings indicates that no date was printed in the edition; the date that follows is the actual date, where known.

ABOUT THE TRANSLATORS

IVOR MONTAGU, *English writer and film producer, studied at the Royal College of Science, London, and King's College, Cambridge. He was one of the founders of the old London Film Society and has served as film critic on four newspapers. He directed silent comedies by H. G. Wells and documentaries made during the Spanish Civil War and World War II, and has edited and been associate producer of early Hitchcock thrillers. He and his wife were members of the Eisenstein group in Hollywood, and he is a co-author (with Eisenstein and G. V. Alexandrov) of the scripts for* Sutter's Gold *and* An American Tragedy. *Mr. Montagu began work on this translation at Eisenstein's request while in an American military hospital in Germany following World War II.*

HERBERT MARSHALL, *who is also English, studied under Eisenstein at the Higher Institute of Cinematography in Moscow and was assistant director to Pudovkin among numerous others in both film and theater there. In England, he founded several theaters, was a director of the Old Vic Company and of the Sadler's Wells Opera Company (1940-41), and has lectured on film and on theater. From 1942-45 he was film adviser to the Russian Ministry of Information and, in later years, a film adviser and producer for the Indian government. Independently, he has produced documentaries as well as children's entertainment films. Mr. Marshall is editor of the 20-volume International Library of Theatre and Cinema (Dennis Dobson Ltd.) and author of* Mayakovsky and His Poetry *(1962).*